convertible
crochet

CUSTOMIZABLE DESIGNS FOR STYLISH GARMENTS

DORIS CHAN

POTTER CRAFT

NEW YORK

You wouldn't expect a Venn diagram of the set of people who are avid crocheters and the set of people who are sci-fi geeks to show much overlap. But that's the intersection where you'll find me as well as all of you others to whom this book is dedicated.

Published in the United States by Potter Craft, an imprint of the Crown Publishing Group, a division of Random House, Inc., New York.

www.crownpublishing.com

www.pottercraft.com

POTTER CRAFT and colophon is a registered trademark of Random House, Inc.

Library of Congress Cataloging-in-Publication Data
Chan, Doris.
  Convertible crochet : customizable designs for stylish garments / Doris Chan.
  Includes index.
1. Crocheting—Patterns. 2. Clothing and dress. I. Title.
  TT825.C383 2013
  746.43'4—dc23
                            2012021120

ISBN 978-0-307-96570-7
eISBN 978-0-307-96571-4

Printed in China

Book and cover design by Karla Baker
Book and cover photographs by Alexandra Grablewski
Technical editing and illustrations by Karen Manthey

10 9 8 7 6 5 4 3 2 1
First Edition

acknowledgments

Hey, Mom, Harry, and Nick! Cookie, please stop barking. Here we go again.

Incalculable thanks to Karen Manthey, illustrator and technical editor extraordinaire. She makes sense of my work. I forever respect and value her input, expertise, and abilities far beyond those of ordinary mortals.

Much inspiration arrived by way of communing with goddesses. Huge, deep thoughts came through crochet whisperer Vashti Braha, whose genius is shared in her DesigningVashti.com newsletter. Thanks, darlin', for the slip stitch education, for the pants thing, and for the Via, fresh lychees, and Emergen-C. Hugs for Diane Moyer, Tammy Hildebrand, and Suzanne Halstead, who are never too busy to lend an ear.

Full marks and credit to Jane Rimmer, the thread crocheter who dared to boldly go where I would not. Her White Dwarf doily sample is brilliant and her words of encouragement were so helpful.

Deep appreciation to my friends and industry contacts who came through with yarn support, no questions asked: Cari Clement and C. S. Carpenter; Stacy Charles, Diane Friedman, and Debbi Skinner at Tahki Stacy Charles; Jocelyn Tunney at Tunney Wool Company; Lisa Myers at Fairmount Fibers; Valerie Teppo at Blue Sky Alpacas; Lori Goldbach at Kraemer Yarns; Karen Carter at Bryson Distributing; Susan Festa at Knitting Fever; Jonelle and Kat at South West Trading Company; and Norah Gaughan at Berroco and Laura Bryant at Prism Yarns.

To my family at Tulip Company, Japan, Ms. Hyomin Kang, Ms. Kazue Ohara, and Mr. Kotaro Harada, I send my greetings and thanks for the awesome tools.

Thanks to my Potter Craft editor, Betty Wong, for her impeccable taste.

In addition to coffee, I am grateful for geeky sci-fi, Pop-Tarts, and, strangely enough, Spam, all of which aided the authoring process.

contents

preface

QUESTION EVERYTHING

There's little doubt that I was a born skeptic. My first word was probably "Why?" followed closely by "Why not?" and must have been in Cantonese, the only language my parents had in common when they married and the one we used at home until I was five. Very quickly the Doris chatter was punctuated with English words and songs I absorbed while mesmerized by television.

My parents must have been relieved to pack their little skeptic off to school every day, if only to provide them a respite from the incessant stream of questions. Mom and Dad did not have much education, at least not by American school standards, so by the time I finished second grade I had gone beyond being able to get answers at home regarding very important stuff about life, the universe, and everything. My parents steered me toward books. At least I was quiet while reading.

Textbooks contained answers but were so boring. I naturally gravitated toward fiction, especially stories about horses and animals. But one series of children's books that imagined an animal in space, Ruthven Todd's *Space Cat*, plunged me into my lifelong romance with science fiction. In that era, the genre was filled with ray guns and hypertestosterone action, appealing more to boys. It wasn't until *A Wrinkle in Time* by Madeleine L'Engle that I found a relatable sci-fi story with a girl as the central character. Granted, Meg Murry was a geeky oddball, but then so was I.

Another influential book was *Flatland: A Romance of Many Dimensions*, the novella by Edwin A. Abbott first published in 1884. On one level *Flatland* is a satiric commentary on the rigid social structure in Victorian England; on another level it takes you on a mind-bending trip to a world with only two dimensions, where men are polygons and women are straight lines, to a closed society where it is heretical, even illegal, for inhabitants to discuss the existence of a third dimension. So what happens when an observer, a sphere from a three-dimensional parallel world, arrives? Imagine how we would react to an extra-dimensional visitor. It wasn't exactly a fun read, but it caused me to view geometry in a totally different light. Way before muggles, there were Flatlanders.

Although I possessed neither the aptitude nor the discipline to go on to study serious science, which demands rigorous proofs grounded in hard-core mathematics, I have always been drawn to the wonder, mystery, and majesty of the great cosmological ideas that are hinted at in my beloved science fiction. Pop science works such as Carl Sagan's *Cosmos* were eye-opening. Is everything connected? Are we truly made of "star stuff," the elements created during the death throes of massive stars in the last infinitesimal fraction of a second before they explode into supernovae? Can it be that space-time is a fabric that folds, bends, and curves and is therefore possible to warp, as in warp drive? All the stuff of science fiction, multiple dimensions, parallel universes, black holes, wormholes, antimatter. For real? Such thoughts not only fueled my imagination, but reinforced the need to question everything, for no great ideas arise unless you look outside the box. In a way, it's the skeptical part of my nature coupled with the romance of science and science fiction that led me to design crochet the way I do and to develop the garments for this book.

WHY NOT?

There are no straight lines or flat surfaces on the human body. In order to create crocheted garments that fit human curves, the traditional approach is to treat crochet as you would dressmaking. In the way fabric is exactingly cut into separate pieces according to a drafted pattern and then sewn together, crocheted garments are usually made by creating separate pieces in specific shapes for front, back, sleeve, collar, and ribbing, and then seaming those pieces together. I began to question the wisdom of this method.

Engineering plain or solid crochet stitches into the necessary pieces for a cut-and-sew type of construction can be accomplished in a fairly straightforward way with increases and decreases at the edges, but doing the same with fancy or complex lace stitches is a nightmare. Why not create internal shaping and avoid the annoying, jarring starts and stops in the flow of the lace?

I never liked seaming crochet. In the process of crocheting, each loop on the hook is intertwined with the next to form stitches, rows of stitches, and columns of rows. Everything is connected. Why can't crocheted garments have that same sense of connectivity and be totally seamless? Or how about developing a set of interchangeable crocheted elements that can be connected into a whole as you go in myriad ways with virtually no seams?

Conventionally, crochet is considered in terms of two dimensions—flatland. We are accustomed to crocheting fabric that lies flat, for example, when we join small squares into big squares and rectangles. We then try making those rectangles cover a three-dimensional form, the human body. Since the medium is yarn and crocheted fabric can be stretchy, the strict rules of geometry do not hold, and it is possible to construct serviceable garments this way.

What about motif shapes beyond the square? Most conventional designs using six-sided and eight-sided motifs (hexagons and octagons) require "filler" motifs, additional little bits that fill in the spaces and allow the shaped motifs to fit together perfectly (tile) into a flat piece. You're still in flatland. Why are pentagons never used? Because pentagons cannot be turned into flat fabric. But, wait. Wouldn't that be a good thing? Why not take advantage of this and use what are essentially two-dimensional crocheted motifs of different shapes and connect them in unconventional ways into flexible fabric that warps and curves on purpose in order to better drape around our three-dimensional bodies?

In the rigid society of seamed garments, what is made to fit your upper body won't fit your lower body. There are few opportunities for alternate uses of the same garment or for swapping, adding, or omitting sections to construct completely different garments. Why not step outside that box and create convertible crochet projects that offer multiple styling, each as happily attractive as the next? Wouldn't it be brilliant if you could transform designs for your own best silhouette and fine-tune the fit to be longer or shorter, to be slim or boxy, to have sleeves or not, to include a collar or not?

If you're asking these same questions and are looking for the unexpected in your crochet, then this book provides some answers for your consideration and experimentation.

introduction

This is the story of Entropy, an original round doily for a new way of thinking about doilies. Like a massive star, from the point at its center to the orbital expanse of lace at its far reaches, Entropy contains all the elements in this book's universe: the ideas, themes, and stitch combinations that reverberate throughout it.

Like a blazing supernova, Entropy explodes and spins out the Spawn of Entropy, a family of twenty-four motifs that are interchangeable, connectable, and adaptable. These motifs, plus the stitch combinations Angular Momentum and Corsair, are the building blocks for all the designs you will find here.

Each of the following four design chapters—Inside the Box, Hey Nineteen, Polygonzo, and Angular Momentum—begins with a flat or straightforward project using the featured motif shape or stitch. As you progress through each chapter, the designs offer techniques to add more and more dimension to your projects, until you've reached maximum curvature with the last garment. The final design chapter, String Theory, sums up all that's been discussed and features garments that offer a multitude of design and styling options.

The convertible pieces found throughout the design chapters are specifically designed to look good and function well however you wear them, as a skirt or as a poncho, upside down or downside up, buttoned and strung or open and loose. Feel absolutely free to style them as you desire. The transformable pieces are the designs you can freely adapt with options for length, add-ons, buttons and strings, collar, peplum, cuffs. Devise your own combination of features for a one-of-a-kind garment that is all your own, because the designs in this book are just the start of your adventure. I expect you to take these tools, expand your skills, and do your own experiments for crochet projects, garments, and accessories that are fresh, multitasking, adjustable for your size, and fun to make.

How to Use This Book

Anyone with solid crochet skills and experience reading and understanding written instructions can make anything in here. It amused me to borrow terms from cosmology in writing about crochet. But don't be put off by the pseudo-techno-gibberish. This is not rocket science.

Before crocheting, please read through the book. Most of the questions you'll have concerning the how-tos and whys are addressed within but might be overlooked if you rush to grab yarn and hook. The most informative and critical of all are the tips and techniques included in the Spawn of Entropy section. You will see those sections referenced again and again throughout the garment patterns as the source of information about making, measuring, managing, joining, finishing, and sizing with motifs.

Many of the convertible designs in this book have what I call a *header*. In traditional thread lace crochet a header is a section, usually a strip or row of plain crochet, along the top of a more elaborate edging or trim that is used for attaching the lace to something else, like a tea towel or linens. Here it refers to the narrow band with holes you'll make around the neck, waist, or arm of a garment. The header is necessary for magic to happen. You'll see.

Many crochet symbol diagrams are included, brilliantly mapping the stitches used for the lace patterns, motifs, and edgings. The master stitch symbol key is given on page 137.

Possibly boring but important is the information at the back of the book that focuses on the beginning and the end, literally. Please make sure to understand chainless foundations (page 140) for the techniques foundation single crochet (fsc) and foundation double crochet (fdc) that are the start of many of my designs. And when you've finished crocheting, you aren't really done until you make friends with BFF, Blocking Friends Forever (page 142).

Other than that, you are clear for launch.

Skill Levels

EASY ● ○ ○

Projects using yarn with basic stitches, repetitive stitch patterns, simple color changes, and simple shaping and finishing.

INTERMEDIATE ● ● ○

Projects using a variety of techniques, such as basic lace patterns or color patterns, and midlevel shaping and finishing.

EXPERIENCED ● ● ●

Projects with intricate stitch patterns, techiques, and dimension, such as nonrepeating patterns, multicolor techniques, fine threads, small hooks, detailed shaping, and refined finishing.

THE ORIGINS OF entropy

Designing an original doily is harder than I imagined. I am rarely called on to engineer a complex round doily from the ground up . . . or from the center point out. Success hinges on devising lace that can be grown at just the right rate of expansion so that each round of crochet contributes to the well-being of the whole. The finished doily should not only lie perfectly flat but also drape well on the body.

I give you Entropy, a spectacular doily round that encompasses four of my favorite lace figures: Copernicus, a wheeled center surrounded by tilted shells; Carina, a pattern of peaked shells; Constellation, an angular pineapple; and Corsair, a pattern of gull-winged sprays. In later chapters these figures morph into stitch patterns and motifs to be employed in surprising ways.

entropy THROW AND SHAWL

The original round crocheted in a soft, cushy yarn turns what might have been fussy lace into carefree style. Entropy intact makes a lacy throw; folded and draped artfully around the shoulders it is a pretty shawl; arranged over a contrasting cloth it makes a bold statement as a topper for an occasional table.

skill level

INTERMEDIATE ● ● ○

Size

45″ (114cm) diameter round

Materials

Berroco Weekend, 75% acrylic, 25% Peruvian cotton, 3½ oz (100g), 205 yd (187m) Medium

4 hanks in 5940 Plum, or approximately 750 yd (686m) medium worsted weight yarn

U.S. Size I-9 (5.5mm) crochet hook or size needed to obtain gauge

Gauge

RND 3: 3¾″ (9.5cm) diameter

Stitch Definitions

SPIKE DTR (SPIKE DOUBLE TRIPLE CROCHET): *This stitch spikes or descends into the chain space 3 rows below, enclosing and gathering 3 chain arches together into the bottom of the dtr.* YO 3 times, insert hook in the ch-sp as indicated 3 rows below, pinching together the 3 chain arches, YO and draw up a loop, [YO and draw through 2 loops on the hook] 4 times.

BOBBLE (DOUBLE CROCHET 3 TOGETHER ALL IN ONE PLACE): YO, insert hook in the next st or sp indicated, YO and draw up a loop, YO and draw through 2 loops on the hook, [YO, insert the hook in the same place, YO and draw up a loop, YO and draw through 2 loops on the hook] 2 times, YO and draw through all 4 loops on the hook.

DC3TOG CLUSTER (DOUBLE CROCHET 3 TOGETHER IN DIFFERENT PLACES): [YO, insert hook in the next stitch indicated, YO and draw up a loop, YO and draw through 2 loops on the hook] 3 times, YO and draw through all 4 loops on the hook.

TR3TOG CLUSTER (TRIPLE CROCHET 3 TOGETHER IN DIFFERENT PLACES): *YO 2 times, insert hook in the next stitch indicated, YO and draw up a loop, [YO and draw through 2 loops on the hook] 2 times*; repeat from * to * 2 times; YO and draw through all 4 loops on the hook.

Pattern Notes

Entropy is crocheted in the traditional doily way, from the center outward, in joined rounds with the right side always facing.

Rounds 1–5 are the Copernicus Section; Rounds 6–10 are the Carina Section; Rounds 11–15 are the Constellation Section; Rounds 16–22 are the Corsair Section; Rounds 23–27 are a reiteration of Constellation.

Instructions

Ch 4 and sl st in the beginning ch to form a ring.

RND 1: Ch 1, 6 sc, sl st in the beginning sc to form a ring—6 sc.

RND 2: Ch 7 *(this equals tr, ch 3)*, tr in the first sc; ch 3, [tr, ch 3] 2 times in each of the next 5 sc; sl st in the 4th ch of the beginning ch—12 ch-3 sps.

RND 3: Ch 1, 4 sc in each of the 12 ch-3 sp; sl st in the beginning sc—48 sc.

RND 4: Ch 3 *(this equals dc)*, skip the first sc; *skip the next sc, dc in the next sc; over the stem of the dc just made, work a petal of [ch 3, 4 dc]; skip the next sc**, dc in the next sc*; repeat from * to * 10 times, then repeat from * to **; sl st in the 3rd ch of the beginning ch—12 petals, 12 dc between the petals.

RND 5: Ch 7 *(this equals dc, ch 4)*; *skip the ch-3 of the next petal, sc in the next dc**; ch 4, skip the remaining 3 dc of the petal, dc in the next dc between the petals; ch 4*; repeat from * to * 10 times, then repeat from * to **; ch 1, dc in the 3rd ch of the beginning ch *(this equals ch 4)*—24 ch-4 sps.

RND 6: Ch 5 *(this equals dc, ch 2)*, sc in the next ch-4 sp; ch 2, *[dc, ch 3, dc] in the next ch-4 sp; ch 2, sc in the next ch-4 sp; ch 2*; repeat from * to * 10 times; dc in beginning sp; ch 1, hdc in the 3rd ch of the beginning ch *(this equals ch 3)*—12 Carina repeats begun.

RND 7: Ch 3, 2 dc in the beginning sp; ch 5, *skip the next (ch 2, sc, ch 2); [3 dc, ch 2, 3 dc] in the next ch-3 sp, ch 5*; repeat from *to * 10 times; 3 dc in the beginning sp; ch 1, sc in the 3rd ch of the beginning ch *(this equals ch 2)*.

ROUNDS 1–16

RND 8: Ch 3, 2 dc in the beginning sp, ch 5; *skip the next ch-5 sp, then [3 dc, ch 2, 3 dc] in the next ch-2 sp, ch 5*; repeat from * to * 10 times; 3 dc in the beginning sp; ch 1, sc in the 3rd ch of the beginning ch *(this equals ch 2)*.

RND 9: Ch 3, 3 dc in the beginning sp, ch 6; *skip the next ch-5 sp, then [4 dc, ch 2, 4 dc] in the next ch-2 sp, ch 6*; repeat from * to * 10 times; 4 dc in the beginning sp; ch 1, sc in the 3rd ch of the beginning ch *(this equals ch 2)*.

RND 10: Ch 1, sc in the beginning sp; *ch 4, [spike dtr, ch 4, spike dtr] in the next ch-5 sp three rows below, ch 4**; [sc, ch 2, sc] in the next ch-2 sp*; repeat from * to * 10 times, then repeat from * to **; sc in the beginning sp; ch 1, sc in the beginning sc *(this equals ch 2)*.

RND 11: Ch 1, sc in the beginning sp, *ch 3, skip the next ch-4 sp, 7 tr in the next ch-4 sp, ch 3; skip the next ch-4 sp, sc in the next ch-2 sp*; repeat from * to * 11 times; on the final repeat, omit the last sc; instead, sl st in the beginning sc—12 Constellation repeats begun.

RND 12: Ch 5 *(this equals dc, ch 2)*, *bobble in the next tr, [ch 1, skip the next tr, bobble in the next tr] 3 times; ch 2**, [dc, ch 3, dc] in the next sc, ch 2*; repeat from * to * 10 times, then repeat from * to **; dc in the beginning sp; ch 1, hdc in the 3rd ch of the beginning ch *(this equals ch 3)*.

RND 13: Ch 1, sc in the beginning sp, *ch 4, sc in the next ch-2 sp; ch 4, bobble in the next ch-1 sp, [ch 1, bobble in the next ch-1 sp] 2 times; ch 4, sc in the next ch-2 sp**; ch 4, sc in the next ch-3 sp*; repeat from * to * 10 times, then repeat from * to **; ch 1, dc in the beginning sc *(this equals ch 4)*.

RND 14: Ch 1, sc in the beginning sp; *[ch 4, sc in the next ch-4 sp] 2 times; ch 4, bobble in the next ch-1 sp, ch 1, bobble in the next ch-1 sp**, [ch 4, sc in the next ch-4 sp] 2 times*; repeat from * to * 10 times, then repeat from * to **; ch 4, sc in the last ch-4 sp; ch 1, dc in the beginning sc *(this equals ch 4)*.

RND 15: Ch 1, sc in the beginning sp, *[ch 4, sc in the next ch-4 sp] 3 times; ch 4, bobble in the next ch-1 sp**; [ch 4, sc in the next ch-4 sp] 2 times*; repeat from * to * 10 times, then repeat from * to **; ch 4, sc in the last ch-4 sp, ch 1, dc in the beginning sc *(this equals ch 4)*.

RND 16: Ch 3, 2 dc in the beginning sp, *(no ch 4 here)* *sc in the next ch-4 sp; ch 4, sc in the next ch-4 sp *(no ch 4 here)***; [3 dc, ch 2, 3 dc] in the next ch-4 sp*; repeat from * to * 22 times, then repeat from * to **; 3 dc in the beginning sp; ch 1, sc in the 3rd ch of the beginning ch *(this equals ch 2)*—24 Corsair repeats begun.

ROUNDS 17-27

RND 17: Ch 3, 2 dc in the beginning sp, *ch 2, sc in the next ch-4 sp, ch 2**; [3 dc, ch 4, 3 dc] in the next ch-2 sp*; repeat from * to * 22 times, then repeat from * to **; 3 dc in the beginning sp; ch 1, dc in the 3rd ch of the beginning ch *(this equals ch 4)*.

RND 18: Ch 5 *(this equals dc, ch 2)*, *dc in each of next 3 stitches; ch 2, skip the next [ch 2, sc, ch 2]; dc in each of the next 3 stitches; ch 2**, [dc, ch 3, dc] in the next ch-4 sp, ch 2*; repeat from * to * 22 times, then repeat from * to **; dc in the beginning sp; ch 1, hdc in the 3rd ch of the beginning ch *(this equals ch 3)*.

NOTE: *The following four rounds (Rnds 19–22) are used in the Add-on Flutter Sleeves (page 136).*

RND 19: Ch 3, 2 dc in the beginning sp, *ch 3; skip next ch-2 sp, dc3tog cluster in the next 3 dc stitches, skip the next ch-2 sp, dc3tog cluster in the next 3 stitches, ch 3; skip the next ch-2 sp**, [3 dc, ch 4, 3 dc] in the next ch-3 sp*; repeat from * to * 22 times, then repeat from * to **; 3 dc in the beginning sp; ch 1, dc in the 3rd ch of the beginning ch *(this equals ch 4)*.

RND 20: Ch 5, *dc in each of the next 3 dc stitches, ch 3; skip the next 2 clusters, then dc in each of next 3 stitches, ch 2**; [dc, ch 3, dc] in the next ch-4 sp, ch 2*; repeat from * to * 22 times, then repeat from * to **; dc in the beginning sp; ch 1, hdc in the 3rd ch of the beginning ch *(this equals ch 3)*.

RND 21: Ch 3, 2 dc in the beginning sp, *ch 3; skip the next ch-2 sp, dc3tog cluster in the next 3 dc stitches, ch 1; skip the next ch-3 sp, then dc3tog cluster in the next 3 stitches, ch 3; skip the next ch-2 sp**, [3 dc, ch 4, 3 dc] in the next ch-3 sp*; repeat from * to * 22 times, then repeat from * to **; 3 dc in the beginning sp; ch 1, dc in the 3rd ch of the beginning ch *(this equals ch 4)*.

RND 22: Ch 5, *dc in each of next 3 dc stitches; ch 4, skip the next 2 clusters, then dc in each of the next 3 stitches; ch 2**, [dc, ch 3, dc] in the next ch-4 sp, ch 2*; repeat from * to * 22 times, then repeat from * to **; dc in beginning sp; dc in the 3rd ch of the beginning ch *(this equals ch 3)*.

RND 23: Ch 4 *(this equals tr)*, 6 tr in the beginning sp, *ch 4, skip the next ch-2 sp, tr3tog cluster in the next 3 dc stitches, ch 2, skip the next ch-4 sp, tr3tog cluster in the next 3 stitches, ch 4, skip the next ch-2 sp**, 7 tr in the next ch-3 sp*; repeat from * to * 22 times, then repeat from * to **; sl st in 4th ch of the beginning ch—24 Constellation repeats begun.

RND 24: Ch 2, dc2tog in the first tr *(this equals a beginning bobble)*, *[ch 1, skip the next tr, bobble in the next tr] 3 times; ch 4, skip the next cluster, [tr, ch 4, tr] in the next ch-2 space**, ch 4, skip the next cluster, bobble in the next tr*; repeat from * to * 22 times, then repeat from * to **; ch 1, dc in the ch-1 stitch at the top of the beginning bobble *(this equals ch 4)*.

RND 25: Ch 1, sc in the beginning sp, *ch 4, skip the next bobble, bobble in the next ch-1 sp, [ch 1, skip the next bobble, bobble in the next ch-1 sp] 2 times, [ch 4, sc in the next ch-4 sp] 3 times*; repeat from * to * 23 times; on the final repeat repeat, omit the last (ch 4, sc); instead, ch 1, dc in the beginning sc *(this equals ch 4)*.

RND 26: Ch 1, sc in the beginning sp, *ch 4, sc in the next ch-4 sp, ch 4, skip the next bobble, bobble in the next ch-1 sp, ch 1, skip the next bobble, bobble in the next ch-1 sp, [ch 4, sc in the next ch-4 sp] 3 times*; repeat from * to * 23 times; on the final repeat, omit the last (ch 4, sc); instead, ch 1, dc in the beginning sc *(this equals ch 4)*.

RND 27: Ch 3, 3 dc in the beginning sp; *(no ch 4 here) [sc in the next ch-4 sp, ch 4] 2 times, skip the next bobble, bobble in the next ch-1 sp, [ch 4, sc in the next ch-4 sp] 2 times, (no ch 4 here)**; [4 dc, ch 4, 4 dc] in the next ch-4 sp*; repeat from * to * 22 times, then repeat from * to **; 4 dc in the beginning sp ; ch 4, sl st in the 3rd ch of the beginning ch. Fasten off.

Weave in the ends, and block.

white dwarf DOILY

I worried what would happen when I gave threadie Jane Rimmer the task of back-engineering big, beefy Entropy into a dainty thread doily. Jane reported that the outer edge occasionally puckered (pulled in) when crocheted in size 10 thread. But with judicious blocking, this makes a lovely flat round.

"White Dwarf is classic! It uses techniques frequently seen in vintage crochet patterns, such as creating joins with a combination of chains and taller stitches. This technique creates smoother joins than slip stitching into the first stitch of the round, and then slip stitching to the middle of the chain loop. This may seem confusing if it's the first time that you've seen the technique, but with a little practice, you will probably love this technique as much as I do."

—Jane

Finished Size

16″ (40.5cm) diameter round

Materials

DMC-Cebelia Crochet Cotton size 10, 100% cotton, 1¾ oz (50g), 284 yd (258.5m) 🔟 Lace/Thread

One ball in White

U.S. Size 7 (1.65mm) steel crochet hook for use with crochet thread

Stitch Definitions

See Entropy (page 11) for stitches and pattern rounds.

Instructions

RNDS 1–27: Make in the same way as Entropy (page 11).

Jane's Tips on Blocking the Doily

Blocking opens the lacework and sets the stitches. Some doilies cup or ruffle and will need a lot of blocking. Normal methods for finishing thread doilies include starching and pinning many points in every row. Happily, White Dwarf needs only a small amount of blocking.

Pin in sections given in the pattern. There are doily templates available online to help block symmetrically. Hold a steam iron several inches above the doily and let the steam penetrate the fibers. Do not press or iron the doily by putting the iron directly on the fabric, which will flatten the beautiful texture that you've worked so hard to create.

tempest SKIRT AND PONCHO

What would happen if you scooped out the center of Entropy and started working the figures around a foundation ring instead? Yes, you'd have a doily with a big hole. But imagine the possibilities when you add a header and drawstring around the hole. In the light worsted/DK gauge shown, you'd have an adult-size skirt or poncho. For a girl's version, experiment with sport weight or even finer yarn.

skill level
INTERMEDIATE ● ● ○

Size

XS (S, M, L, XL), sample shown is size XS

Finished waist/neck 26½ (29, 32, 34½, 37)" (67 [74, 81, 88, 94]cm) with plenty of stretch to pull on; hip 45 (49½, 54, 58½, 63)" (114 [126, 137, 149, 160]cm); length 22" (56cm)

Materials

Blue Sky Alpacas Skinny Dyed, 100% organic cotton, 2¼ oz (65g), 150 yd (137m) (**3**) Light

5 (6, 6, 7, 8) hanks in #31 Clay

U.S. Size I-9 (5.5mm) crochet hook or size needed to obtain gauge

Gauge

12 fsc = 4" (10cm)

In Eshell stitch pattern, one repeat (from center of shell to center of next shell) = 3¼" (8cm)

RND 4: total depth Eshell stitch pattern (including foundation) = 3" (7.5cm)

Stitch Definitions

FSC (FOUNDATION SINGLE CROCHET): See Chainless Foundations (page 140).

EDC (EXTENDED DOUBLE CROCHET): YO, insert hook in next stitch as indicated, YO and draw up a loop, YO and draw through one loop on hook, [YO, draw through 2 loops on hook] 2 times.

ESHELL (EXTENDED DC-DC-DC SHELL): *This is a 3-stitch shell with an Edc as the first arm, then two dc made in the chain at the base of the Edc.*

Edc in st or sp indicated, YO, insert the hook in the ch at the base of the Edc just made, *YO and draw up a loop, [YO and draw through 2 loops on the hook] 2 times*; YO, insert the hook in the same ch at the base of the Edc, repeat from * to * for the second dc.

See Entropy (page 11) for stitches and pattern rounds.

Pattern Notes

Tempest is crocheted in the traditional doily way, from a center foundation outward, in joined rounds with the right side always facing.

The Eshell stitch pattern of the yoke is similar to Angular Momentum (page 98), except worked in rounds here instead of rows.

For a longer garment, see the tip (page 18) for adding rounds to the yoke.

For a shorter garment, it is not practical to omit rounds in the yoke. You may choose to lighten the hem a couple inches by stopping before the last five rounds of Constellation points. Work through Tempest Rnd 20, then complete the Corsair section with the finishing rounds found in the Add-on Flutter Sleeves, Rnds 8–9 (page 136).

SKIRT YOKE

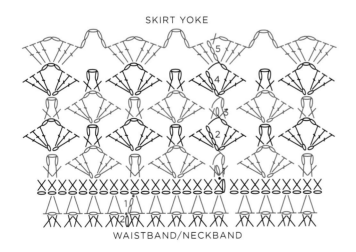

WAISTBAND/NECKBAND

Instructions

Fsc 80 (88, 96, 104, 112); bring the ends of the foundation together, being careful not to twist the stitches. Sl st in the beginning sc to form a ring, then begin to work across the sc edge. Create 10 (11, 12, 13, 14) Eshell stitch pattern repeats.

RND 1: Ch 1, sc in first sc; *skip the next 3 sc, [Eshell, ch 3, Eshell] in the next sc; skip the next 3 sc**, [sc, ch 3, sc] in the next sc*; repeat from * to * 8 (9, 10, 11, 12) times, then repeat from * to **; sc in the beginning sc; ch 1, hdc in the beginning sc *(this equals ch 3)*—20 (22, 24, 26, 28) ch-3 sps.

RND 2: Ch 4, 2 dc in the 4th ch from the hook *(this equals a beginning Eshell)*; *[sc, ch 3, sc] in the next ch-3 sp *(between shells)***, [Eshell, ch 3, Eshell] in the next ch-3 sp (between the single crochet stitches)*; repeat from * to * 8 (9, 10, 11, 12) times, then repeat from * to **; Eshell in the beginning sp; ch 1, hdc in the 4th ch of the beginning ch *(this equals ch 3)*.

RND 3: Ch 1, sc in the beginning sp; *[Eshell, ch 3, Eshell] in the next ch-3 sp**; [sc, ch 3, sc] in the next ch-3 sp*; repeat from * to * 8 (9, 10, 11, 12) times, then repeat from * to **; sc in the beginning sp; ch 1, hdc in the beginning sc *(this equals ch 3)*.

TIP: *For a deeper skirt yoke, repeat Rnds 2–3 for desired length.*

RND 4: Repeat Rnd 2.

RND 5: Ch 3, 2 dc in the beginning sp; *[ch 5, skip next (sc, ch 3, and sc)]**, [3 dc, ch 2, 3 dc] in the next ch-3 sp*; repeat from * to * 8 (9, 10, 11, 12) times, then repeat from * to **; 3 dc in the beginning sp; ch 1, sc in the 3rd ch of the beginning ch *(this equals ch 2)*—10 (11, 12, 13, 14) Carina repeats begun.

RNDS 6–25: Work Rounds 8–27 of Entropy (page 13), adjusting the number of pattern repeats according to your size. Fasten off.

Finishing
HEADER

With the right side facing, return to the foundation round. Join new yarn with a slip stitch in any chain of the foundation where there are already stitches in the sc edge—in other words, not in one of the skipped stitches.

RND 1: Ch 3 *(this equals hdc, ch 1)*, hdc in the same st, *skip the next ch, [hdc, ch 1, hdc] in the next ch*; repeat from * to * around; sl st in the 2nd ch of the beginning ch—40 (44, 48, 52, 56) ch-1 sps.

RND 2: Ch 1, 2 sc in each ch-1 sp around; sl st in the beginning sc. Fasten off—80 (88, 96, 104, 112) sc.

Weave in the ends, and block.

String

Choose a string (page 137) type as desired, and make one string 45" (114cm) in length or to taste. Use a smaller hook, if necessary, for a firm texture.

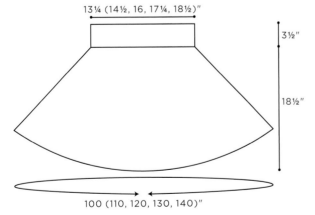

13¼ (14½, 16, 17¼, 18½)"

3½"

18½"

100 (110, 120, 130, 140)"

Copernicus Minor Pent

Copernicus Major Pent

Copernicus Major Oct

Copernicus Minor

Copernicus Major Square

Copernicus Minor Hex

Copernicus Minor Square

SPAWN OF ENTROPY: motifs

By pulling out three recurring lace figures and framing them, we can capture bits of Entropy as motifs, like snapshots in a family photo album. There's no need to read the stitch-by-stitch instructions below until you're ready to crochet one of the motif-driven designs, but here is the place to revisit for the complete catalog of twenty-four motifs, named by Style, Class, and Configuration, along with tips for a happy playtime.

Style

Copernicus is taken from the very center of Entropy. It is a tilt-a-whirl of petals orbiting a spoked wheel.

Carina features a pattern of pointy shells like arrow heads, launched from bow strings formed by spiked stitches.

Constellation is cousin to the pineapple. In the square and oct configurations, Constellation appears more floral; it is in the pent and hex configurations that it lives up to its name and resembles a star.

Class

The difference between minor and major class motifs is in the number of rounds. Major motifs have an extra round of ch-4 spaces inserted before the last round. Having two classes of motifs is useful for matching gauge and dimensions when altering proportions or swapping yarns, and is critical for sizing many of the garment designs.

Configuration

I offer four configurations of regular polygons: square, pent, hex, and oct, containing four, five, six, and eight equal sides and angles, respectively.

Skill Level

The skill level of the motifs is sort of Easy. I know the instructions have lots of words and alien images. A civilian (aka noncrocheting) friend tells me the diagrams look like demented crop circles. These motifs might be a challenge for newbie crocheters, but they ain't rocket science. If you've had run-ins with motifs other than granny squares or if you grok the language of crochet symbols, then you'll be well prepared. What kicks some of the later garment projects up to Intermediate and Experienced is the complexity of the assembly and finishing. Even then, if you enjoy puzzles, or better still, if you are an ace at Tetris, then you're good to go.

Pattern Notes

Although the three lace centers are very different from one another, there's a certain sameness to the outer rounds that frame these motifs. That's the beauty part. You'll appreciate the reason when you get to Universal Assembly (page 33).

All motifs are crocheted in the traditional doily way, in joined rounds with the right side always facing. Rather than nail it down to the same spot every time, it is handy to jockey the beginning/ending of each round to the location that best prepares you for the next round. This shifting of the join makes the "seam" less bulky, more attractive, or better disguised, with less slip stitching forward into the new round in order to get where you need to be. Often rounds end in the center of a chain space. For example, the ending "ch 1, dc in the 3rd ch of the beginning ch" is equal to a ch 4. The remaining loop on the hook is located at the middle of the arch. As you start the new round, the *beginning space* is the big hole under the stem of that last closing stitch.

The garment patterns will tell you the (style, class, and configuration) motifs required, along with yarn, hook, and gauge needed to make a project. What follows here are the general motif instructions to plug and play.

Copernicus Motifs
COPERNICUS SQUARES: CENTER ROUNDS

Ch 4; sl st in the beginning ch to form a ring.

RND 1: Ch 6 *(this equals dc, ch 3)*, [dc, ch 3] 7 times in the ring; sl st in the 3rd ch of the beginning ch—8 ch-3 sps.

RND 2: Ch 1, 4 sc in each ch-3 sps; sl st in the first sc—32 sc.

RND 3: Ch 3 *(this equals dc)*, skip first sc, [skip the next sc, dc in the next sc; then, over the stem of the dc just made, work a petal of (ch 3, 4 dc); skip the next sc, dc in the next sc] 8 times; on the final repeat, omit the last dc; instead, sl st in the 3rd ch of the beginning ch—8 petals, 8 dc between the petals.

RND 4: Ch 7 *(this equals dc, ch 4)*; [skip the ch-3 of the next petal, sc in the next dc; ch 4, skip the remaining 3 dc of the petal, dc in the next dc between the petals, ch 4] 7 times; skip the ch-3 of the last petal, sc in the next dc;

skip the remaining 3 dc of the petal, ch 1, dc in the 3rd ch of the beginning ch *(this equals ch 4)*—16 ch-4 sps.

Copernicus Minor Square: Last Round

RND 5: Ch 1, sc in the beginning space; *(no ch-4 here)* [4 dc, ch 4 (or join), 4 dc] in the next ch-4 sp; *(no ch-4 here)* sc in the next ch-4 sp; [ch 4 (or join), sc in the next ch-sp] 2 times*; repeat from * to * 3 times; on the final repeat, omit the last sc; instead, sl st in the beginning sc. Fasten off.

Copernicus Major Square: Last Rounds

RND 5: Ch 1, sc in the beginning sp; *ch 4, (sc, ch 4, sc) in the next ch-sp; [ch 4, sc in the next ch-sp] 3 times*; repeat from * to * 3 times; on the final repeat, omit the last (ch 4, sc); instead, ch 1, dc in the beginning sc—20 ch-4 sps.

RND 6: Ch 1, sc in the beginning sp; *ch 4 (or join), sc in the next ch-sp; *(no ch-4 here)* [4 dc, ch 4 (or join), 4 dc] in the next ch-4 sp; *(no ch-4 here)* sc in the next ch-sp; [ch 4 (or join), sc in the next ch-sp] 2 times*; repeat from * to * 3 times; on the final repeat, omit the last sc; instead, sl st in the beginning sc. Fasten off.

COPERNICUS PENTS: CENTER ROUNDS

Ch 5; sl st in the first ch to form a ring.

RND 1: Ch 1, 10 sc in the ring; sl st in the beginning sc—10 sc.

RND 2: Ch 6 *(this equals dc, ch 3)*, skip the first sc, [dc, ch 3] in each of the 9 sc; sl st in the 3rd ch of the beginning ch—10 ch-3 sps.

RND 3: Ch 1, 4 sc in each of the 10 ch-3 sps; sl st in the beginning sc—40 sc.

COPERNICUS MINOR SQUARE

COPERNICUS MAJOR SQUARE

COPERNICUS MINOR PENT

COPERNICUS MAJOR PENT

RND 4: Ch 3 (this equals dc), skip the first sc, [skip next sc, dc in the next sc; over the stem of the dc just made, work a petal of (ch 3, 4 dc); skip the next sc, dc in next sc] 10 times; on the final repeat, omit the last dc; instead, sl st in the 3rd ch of the beginning ch—10 petals, 10 dc between the petals.

RND 5: Ch 7 (this equals dc, ch 4); [skip the ch-3 of the petal, sc in the next dc, ch 4; skip the remaining 3 dc of the petal, dc in the next dc between the petals, ch 4] 9 times; skip the ch-3 of the last petal and sc in the next dc; skip the remaining 3 dc of the petal; ch 1, dc in the 3rd ch of the beginning ch (this equals ch 4)—20 ch-4 sps.

Copernicus Minor Pent: Last Round

RND 6: Ch 1, sc in the beginning sp; *(no ch-4 here) [4 dc, ch 4 (or join), 4 dc] in the next ch-4 sp; (no ch-4 here) sc in the next ch-sp; [ch 4 (or join), sc in the next ch-sp] 2 times*; repeat from * to * 4 times; on the final repeat, omit the last sc; instead, sl st in the beginning sc. Fasten off.

Copernicus Major Pent: Last Rounds

RND 6: Ch 1, sc in the beginning sp; *ch 4, (sc, ch 4, sc) in the next ch-sp; [ch 4, sc in next ch-sp] 3 times*; repeat from * to * 4 times; on the final repeat, omit the last [ch 4, sc]; instead, ch 1, dc in the beginning sc—25 ch-4 sps.

RND 7: Ch 1, sc in the beginning sp; *ch 4 (or join), sc in the next ch-sp; (no ch-4 here) [4 dc, ch 4 (or join), 4 dc] in the next ch-4 sp; (no ch-4 here) sc in the next ch-sp; [ch 4 (or join), sc in the next ch-sp] 2 times*; repeat from * to * 4 times; on the final repeat, omit the last sc; instead, sl st in the beginning sc. Fasten off.

COPERNICUS HEXES: CENTER ROUNDS

RND 1: Ch 2, 6 sc in the 2nd ch from the hook; sl st in the first sc to make a ring—6 sc.

RND 2: Ch 7 (this equals tr, ch 3), tr in the first sc; [ch 3, tr] 2 times in each of the next 5 sc; [ch 3, sl st] in the 4th ch of the beginning ch—12 ch-3 sps.

RND 3: Ch 1, 4 sc in each of the 12 ch-3 sps; sl st in the beginning sc—48 sc.

RND 4: Ch 3 (this equals dc), skip the first sc, [skip the next sc, dc in the next sc; over the stem of the dc just made, work a petal of (ch 3, 4 dc); skip next sc, dc in the next sc] 12 times; on the final repeat, omit the last dc; instead, sl st in the 3rd ch of the beginning ch—12 petals, 12 dc between the petals.

RND 5: Ch 7 (this equals dc, ch 4), [skip the ch-3 of the next petal, sc in the next dc; ch 4, skip the remaining 3 dc of the petal, dc in the next dc between the petals, ch 4] 11 times; skip the ch-3 of the last petal, sc in the next dc, skip the remaining 3 dc of the petal, ch 1, dc in the 3rd ch of the beginning ch—24 ch-4 sps.

Copernicus Minor Hex: Last Round

RND 6: Ch 1, sc in the beginning sp; *(no ch-4 here) [4 dc, ch 4 (or join), 4 dc] in the next ch-4 sp; (no ch-4 here) sc in the next ch-sp; [ch 4 (or join), sc in the next ch-sp] 2 times*; repeat from * to * 5 times; on the final repeat, omit the last sc; instead, sl st in the beginning sc. Fasten off.

Copernicus Major Hex: Last Rounds

RND 6: Ch 1, sc in the beginning sp; *ch 4, (sc, ch 4, sc) in next ch-sp; [ch 4, sc in the next ch-sp] 3 times*; repeat from * to * 5 times; on the final repeat, omit the last (ch 4, sc); instead, ch 1, dc in the beginning sc—30 ch-4 sps.

COPERNICUS MINOR HEX

COPERNICUS MAJOR HEX

RND 3: Ch 3 *(this equals dc)*, skip the first sc, [skip the next sc, dc in the next stitch; over the stem of the dc just made, work a petal of (ch 3, 4 dc); skip the next sc, dc in the next sc] 8 times; on the final repeat, omit the last dc; instead, sl st in the 3rd ch of the beginning ch—8 petals, 8 dc between the petals.

RND 4: Ch 7 *(this equals dc, ch 4)*, [skip the ch-3 of the next petal, sc in the next dc; ch 4, skip the remaining 3 dc of the petal, dc in the dc between the petals, ch 4] 8 times; on the final repeat, omit the last dc; instead, sl st in the 3rd ch of the beginning ch—16 ch-4 sps.

RND 5: Ch 1, 4 sc in each of the 16 ch-4 sps; sl st in the beginning sc—64 sc.

RND 6: Ch 3, skip the first sc, [skip the next sc, dc in the next sc; over the stem of the dc just made, work (ch 3, 4 dc); skip the next sc, dc in the next sc] 16 times; on the final repeat, omit the last dc; instead, sl st in the 3rd ch of the beginning ch—16 petals, 16 dc between the petals.

RND 7: Ch 7, [skip the ch-3 of the next petal, sc in the next dc; ch 4, skip the remaining 3 dc stitches of the petal; dc in the dc between the petals, ch 4] 15 times; skip the ch-3 stitches of the last petal, sc in the next dc; skip the remaining 3 dc of the petal; ch 1, dc in the 3rd ch of the beginning ch *(this equals ch 4)*—32 ch-4 sps.

Copernicus Minor Oct: Last Round

RND 8: Ch 1, sc in the beginning sp; *(no ch-4 here)* [4 dc, ch 4 (or join), 4 dc] in the next ch-4 sp; *(no ch-4 here)* sc in the next ch-sp; [ch 4 (or join), sc in the next ch-sp] 2 times*; repeat from * to * 7 times; on the last repeat, omit the last sc; instead, sl st in the beginning sc. Fasten off.

Copernicus Major Oct: Last Rounds

RND 8: Ch 1, sc in the beginning sp; *ch 4, (sc, ch 4, sc) in the next ch-sp; [ch 4, sc in the next ch-sp] 3 times*; repeat from * to * 7 times; on the final repeat, omit the last (ch 4, sc); instead, ch 1, dc in the beginning sc *(this equals ch 4)*—40 ch-4 sps.

RND 9: Ch 1, sc in the beginning sp; *ch 4 (or join), sc in the next ch-sp; *(no ch-4 here)* [4 dc, ch 4 (or join), 4 dc] in the next ch-4 sp; *(no ch-4 here)* sc in the next ch-sp; [ch 4 (or join), sc in the next ch-sp] 2 times*; repeat from * to * 7 times; on the final repeat, omit the last sc; instead, sl st in the beginning sc. Fasten off.

RND 7: Ch 1, sc in the beginning sp; *ch 4 (or join), sc in the next ch-sp; *(no ch-4 here)* [4 dc, ch 4 (or join), 4 dc] in the next ch-4 sp; *(no ch-4 here)*, sc in the next ch-sp; [ch 4 (or join), sc in the next ch-sp] 2 times*; repeat from * to * 5 times; on the final repeat, omit the last sc; instead, sl st in the beginning sc. Fasten off.

COPERNICUS OCTS: CENTER ROUNDS

Ch 4, sl st in the beginning ch to form a ring.

RND 1: Ch 6 *(this equals dc, ch 3)*, [dc, ch 3] 7 times in the ring; sl st in the 3rd ch of the beginning ch—8 ch-3 sps.

RND 2: Ch 1, 4 sc in each of the next 8 ch-3 sps; sl st in the beginning sc—32 sc.

COPERNICUS MINOR OCT

COPERNICUS MAJOR OCT

Carina Motifs

Stitch Definitions

SPIKE TR (SPIKE TRIPLE CROCHET): *This stitch spikes or descends into the chain space 2 rows below, enclosing and gathering 2 chain arches together into the bottom of the triple crochet.*

YO 2 times, insert the hook in ch-sp as indicated 2 rows below, pinching together the 2 chain arches; YO and draw up a loop, [YO and draw through the 2 loops on the hook] 3 times.

SPIKE DTR (SPIKE DOUBLE TRIPLE CROCHET): *This stitch spikes or descends into the chain space 3 rows below, enclosing and gathering 3 chain arches together into the bottom of the dtr.*

YO 3 times, insert the hook in ch-sp as indicated 3 rows below, pinching together the 3 chain arches; YO and draw up a loop, [YO and draw through the 2 loops on the hook] 4 times.

CARINA SQUARES: CENTER ROUNDS

Ch 4; sl st in the beginning ch to form a ring.

RND 1: Ch 6 *(this equals dc, ch 3)*, [dc in the ring, ch 3] 6 times; dc in the ring; ch 1, hdc in the 3rd ch of the beginning ch *(this equals ch 3)*—8 ch-3 sps.

RND 2: Ch 3, 3 dc in the beginning sp; ch 2, [skip the next ch-3 sp, (4 dc, ch 2, 4 dc) in the next ch-3 sp, ch 2] 3 times; 4 dc in the beginning sp; ch 1, sc in the 3rd ch of the beginning ch *(this equals ch 2)*.

RND 3: Ch 1, sc in the beginning sp; *ch 4, [spike tr, ch 4, spike tr] in the next ch-3 sp 2 rows below; ch 4**, (sc, ch

2, sc) in the next ch-2 sp*; repeat from * to * 2 times, then repeat from * to **; sc in the beginning sp; ch 1, sc in the beginning sc.

Carina Minor Square: Last Round

RND 4: Ch 1, sc in the beginning sp; *ch 4 (or join), sc in the next ch-4 sp; *(no ch 4 here)* [4 dc, ch 4 (or join), 4 dc] in the next ch-4 sp; *(no ch 4 here)* sc in the next ch-4 sp;

ch 4 (or join), sc in the next ch-2 sp*; repeat from * to * 3 times; on the final repeat, omit the last sc; instead, sl st in the beginning sc. Fasten off.

Carina Major Square: Last Rounds

RND 4: Ch 1, sc in the beginning sp; *ch 4, sc in the next ch-4 sp; ch 4, [sc, ch 4, sc] 2 times in the next ch-4 sp; ch 4, sc in the next ch-4 sp**; ch 4, sc in the next ch-2 sp*; repeat from * to * 2 times, then repeat from * to **; ch 1, dc in the beginning sc (*this equals ch 4*)—20 ch-4 sps.

RND 5: Ch 1, sc in the beginning sp; *[ch 4 (or join), sc in the next ch-4 sp] 2 times; *(no ch 4 here)* [4 dc, ch 4 (or join), 4 dc] in the next ch-4 sp; *(no ch 4 here)* sc in the next ch-4 sp; ch 4 (or join), sc in the next ch-4 sp*; repeat from * to * 3 times; on the final repeat, omit the last sc; instead, sl st in the beginning sc. Fasten off.

CARINA PENTS: CENTER ROUNDS

Ch 6; sl st in the beginning ch to form a ring.

RND 1: Ch 3 *(this equals dc)*, 2 dc in the ring; [ch 2, 3 dc in the ring] 4 times; ch 1, sc in the 3rd ch of the beginning ch *(this equals ch 2)*—5 ch-2 sps.

RND 2: Ch 3, 2 dc in the beginning sp; ch 2, [(3 dc, ch 2, 3 dc) in the next ch-2 sp, ch 2] 4 times; 3 dc in the beginning sp; ch 1, sc in the 3rd ch of the beginning ch.

RND 3: Ch 3, 3 dc in the beginning sp; ch 4, skip the next ch-2 sp, [(4 dc, ch 2, 4 dc) in the next ch-2 sp; ch 4, skip the next ch-2 sp] 4 times; 4 dc in the beginning sp; ch 1, sc in the 3rd ch of the beginning ch.

CARINA MINOR PENT

CARINA MINOR SQUARE

CARINA MAJOR SQUARE

CARINA MAJOR PENT

CARINA MINOR HEX

CARINA MAJOR HEX

RND 4: Ch 1, sc in the beginning sp; [ch 4, (spike tr, ch 4, spike tr) in the next ch-2 sp 2 rows below; ch 4, (sc, ch 2, sc) in the next ch-2 sp] 5 times; on the final repeat, omit the last [sc, ch 2, sc]; instead, sc in the beginning sp; ch 1, sc in the beginning sc.

Carina Minor Pent: Last Round

RND 5: Ch 1, sc in the beginning sp; *ch 4 (or join), sc in the next ch-4 sp; *(no ch 4 here)* [4 dc, ch 4 (or join), 4 dc] in the next corner ch-4 sp; *(no ch 4 here)* sc in the next ch-4 sp; ch 4 (or join), sc in the next ch-2 sp*; repeat from * to * 4 times; on the final repeat, omit the last sc; instead, sl st in the beginning sc. Fasten off.

Carina Major Pent: Last Rounds

RND 5: Ch 1, sc in the beginning sp; *ch 4, sc in the next ch-4 sp; ch 4, (sc, ch 4, sc) in the next ch-4 sp; ch 4, sc in the next ch-4 sp**; ch 4, sc in the next ch-2 sp*; repeat from * to * 3 times, then repeat from * to **; ch 1, dc in the beginning sc *(this equals ch 4)*.

RND 6: Ch 1, sc in the beginning sp; *[ch 4 (or join), sc in the next ch-4 sp] 2 times; *(no ch 4 here)* [4 dc, ch 4 (or join), 4 dc] in the next ch-4 sp; *(no ch 4 here)* sc in the next ch-4 sp; ch 4 (or join), sc in the next ch-4 sp*; repeat from * to * 4 times; on the final repeat, omit the last sc; instead, sl st in the beginning sc. Fasten off.

CARINA HEXES: CENTER ROUNDS

Ch 8; sl st in the beginning ch to form a ring.

RND 1: Ch 4 *(this equals tr)*, 2 tr in the ring; [ch 2, 3 tr in the ring] 5 times; ch 1, sc in the 4th ch of the beginning ch *(this equals ch 2)*—6 ch-2 sps.

RND 2: Ch 3, 2 dc in the beginning sp; ch 2, [(3 dc, ch 2, 3 dc) in the next ch-2 sp, ch 2] 5 times; 3 dc in the beginning sp; ch 1, sc in the 3rd ch of the beginning ch *(this equals ch 2)*.

RND 3: Ch 3, 3 dc in the beginning sp; ch 4, skip the next ch-2 sp; [(4 dc, ch 2, 4 dc) in the next ch-2 sp; ch 4, skip the next ch-2 sp] 5 times; 4 dc in the beginning sp; ch 1, sc in the 3rd ch of the beginning ch.

RND 4: Ch 1, sc in the beginning sp; [ch 4, (spike tr, ch 4, spike tr) in the next ch-2 sp 2 rows below; ch 4, (sc, ch 2, sc) in the next ch-2 sp] 6 times; on the final repeat, omit the last (sc, ch 2, sc); instead, sc in the beginning sp; ch 1, sc in the beginning sc.

Carina Minor Hex: Last Round

RND 5: Ch 1, sc in the beginning sp; *ch 4 (or join), sc in the next ch-4 sp; *(no ch 4 here)* [4 dc, ch 4 (or join), 4 dc] in the next ch-4 sp; *(no ch 4 here)* sc in the next ch-4 sp; ch 4 (or join), sc in the next ch-2 sp*; repeat from * to * 5 times; on the final repeat, omit the last sc; instead, sl st in the beginning sc. Fasten off.

Carina Major Hex: Last Rounds

RND 5: Ch 1, sc in the beginning sp; *ch 4, sc in the next ch-4 sp; ch 4, (sc, ch 4, sc) in the next ch-4 sp; ch 4, sc in the next ch-4 sp**; ch 4, sc in the next ch-2 sp*; repeat from * to * 4 times, then repeat from * to **; ch 1, dc in the beginning sc.

RND 6: Ch 1, sc in the beginning sp; *[ch 4 (or join), sc in the next ch-4 sp] 2 times; *(no ch 4 here)* [4 dc, ch 4 (or join), 4 dc] in the next ch-4 sp; *(no ch 4 here)* sc in the next ch-4 sp; ch 4 (or join), sc in the next ch-4 sp*; repeat from * to * 5 times; on the final repeat, omit the last sc; instead, sl st in the beginning sc. Fasten off.

CARINA MINOR OCT

CARINA MAJOR OCT

CARINA OCT: CENTER ROUNDS

Ch 6; sl st in the beginning ch to form a ring.

RND 1: Ch 3 *(this equals dc)*, 15 dc in the ring; sl st in the 3rd ch of the beginning ch—16 dc.

RND 2: Ch 4 *(this equals tr)*, 2 tr in the first dc; [ch 3, skip the next dc, 3 tr in the next dc] 7 times; ch 1, hdc in the 4th ch of the beginning ch *(this equals ch 3)*—8 ch-3 sps.

RND 3: Ch 3, 2 dc in the beginning sp; [ch 4, (3 dc, ch 2, 3 dc) in the next ch-3 sp] 7 times; ch 4, 3 dc in beginning sp; ch 1, sc in the 3rd ch of the beginning ch *(this equals ch 2)*.

RND 4: Ch 3, 2 dc in the beginning sp; ch 4, skip next ch-4 sp; [(3 dc, ch 2, 3 dc) in next ch-2 sp; ch 4, skip the next ch-4 sp] 7 times; 3 dc in the beginning sp; ch 1, sc in the 3rd ch of the beginning ch.

RND 5: Ch 3, 3 dc in the beginning sp; ch 5, skip the next ch-4 sp, [(4 dc, ch 2, 4 dc) in the next ch-2 sp; ch 5, skip the next ch-4 sp] 7 times; 4 dc in the beginning sp; ch 1, sc in the 3rd ch of the beginning ch.

RND 6: Ch 1, sc in the beginning sp; [ch 4, (spike dtr, ch 4, spike dtr) in the next ch-4 sp 3 rows below; ch 4, (sc, ch 2, sc) in the next ch-2 sp] 8 times; on the final repeat, omit the last (sc, ch 2, sc); instead, sc in the beginning sp; ch 1, sc in the beginning sc.

Carina Minor Oct: Last Round

RND 7: Ch 1, sc in the beginning sp; *ch 4 (or join), sc in the next ch-4 sp; *(no ch 4 here)* [4 dc, ch 4 (or join), 4 dc] in the next ch-4 sp; *(no ch 4 here)* sc in the next ch-4 sp; ch 4 (or join), sc in next ch-2 sp*; repeat from * to * 7 times; on the final repeat, omit the last sc; instead, sl st in the beginning sc. Fasten off.

Carina Major Oct: Last Rounds

RND 7: Ch 1, sc in the beginning sp; *ch 4, (sc, ch 4, sc) in the next ch-4 sp; ch 4, [sc, ch 4] 2 times in the next ch-4 sp; ch 4, sc in the next ch-4 sp**; ch 4, sc in the next ch-2 sp*; repeat from * to * 6 times, then repeat from * to **; ch 1, dc in the beginning sc *(this equals ch 4)*.

RND 8: Ch 1, sc in the beginning sp; *[ch 4 (or join), sc in the next ch-4 sp] 2 times; *(no ch 4 here)* [4 dc, ch 4 (or join), 4 dc] in the next ch-4 sp; *(no ch 4 here)* sc in the next ch-4 sp; ch 4 (or join), sc in the next ch-4 sp*; repeat from * to * 7 times; on the final repeat, omit the last sc; instead, sl st in the beginning sc. Fasten off.

Constellation Motifs

Stitch Definitions

DC2TOG (DOUBLE CROCHET 2 TOGETHER ALL IN ONE PLACE): YO, insert the hook in the next st or sp as indicated, YO and draw up a loop; YO and draw through the 2 loops on the hook; YO, insert the hook in the same place, YO and draw up a loop; YO and draw through the 2 loops on the hook; YO and draw through all 3 loops on the hook.

BOBBLE (DOUBLE CROCHET 3 TOGETHER ALL IN ONE PLACE): YO, insert the hook in next st or sp as indicated, YO and draw up a loop; YO and draw through the 2 loops on the hook; [YO, insert the hook in the same place, YO and draw up a loop; YO and draw through the 2 loops on the hook] 2 times; YO and draw through all 4 loops on the hook.

CONSTELLATION SQUARES: CENTER ROUNDS

Ch 5; sl st in the beginning ch to form a ring.

RND 1: Ch 2 *(this equals hdc)*, 19 hdc in the ring; sl st in the 2nd ch of the beginning ch—20 hdc.

RND 2: Ch 2, dc2tog in the same ch *(this equals a beginning bobble)*; *[ch 1, skip the next hdc, bobble in the next hdc] 2 times; ch 4, *(do not skip here)* make a bobble in the next hdc*; repeat from * to * 3 times; on the final repeat, omit the last bobble; instead, sl st in the top loops of the ch-1 following the beginning bobble—12 bobbles, 4 ch-4 sps.

RND 3: Ch 2, dc2tog in the beginning ch-1 sp *(this equals a beginning bobble)*; *ch 1, make a bobble in the next ch-1 sp; ch 4, (dc, ch 4, dc) in the next ch-4 sp; ch 4, make a bobble in the next chain-1 sp*; repeat from * to * 3 times; on the final repeat, omit the last bobble; instead, sl st in the top loops of the chain-1 following the beginning bobble.

Constellation Minor Square: Last Round

RND 4: Ch 2, dc2tog in the beginning ch-1 sp *(this equals a beginning bobble)*; *ch 4 (or join), sc in the next ch-4 sp; *(no ch 4 here)* [4 dc, ch 4 (or join), 4 dc] in the next ch-4 sp; *(no ch 4 here)* sc in the next ch-4 sp; ch 4 (or join), make a bobble in the next ch-1 sp*; repeat from * to * 3 times; on the final repeat, omit the last bobble; instead, sl st in the top loops of the chain-1 following the beginning bobble. Fasten off.

Constellation Major Square: Last Rounds

RND 4: Ch 2, dc2tog in the beginning ch-1 sp, *ch 4, sc in the next ch-4 sp (sc, ch 4, sc) in the next ch-4 sp; ch 4, sc in the next ch-4 sp**; ch 4, make a bobble in the next ch-1 sp*; repeat from * to * 2 times, then repeat from * to **; ch 1, dc in the top loops of the ch-1 that closes the beginning bobble—20 ch-4 sps.

RND 5: Ch 1, sc in the beginning sp; *[ch 4 (or join), sc in the next ch-4 sp] 2 times; *(no ch 4 here)* [4 dc, ch 4 (or join), 4 dc] in the next ch-4 sp; *(no ch 4 here)* sc in the

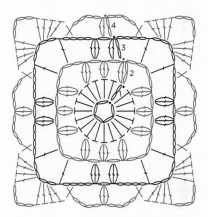

CONSTELLATION MINOR SQUARE

CONSTELLATION MAJOR SQUARE

next ch-4 sp; ch 4 (or join), sc in the next ch-4 sp*; repeat from * to * 3 times; on the final repeat, omit the last sc; instead, sl st in the beginning sc. Fasten off.

CONSTELLATION PENTS: CENTER ROUNDS

Ch 6; sl st in the beginning ch to form a ring.

RND 1: Ch 4 *(this equals tr)*, 24 tr in the ring; sl st in the 4th ch of the beginning ch—25 tr.

RND 2: Ch 2, dc2tog in the first tr *(this equals a beginning bobble)*; *[ch 1, skip the next stitch, make a bobble in the next stitch] 2 times; ch 5, *(do not skip here)* make a bobble in the next stitch*; repeat from * to * 4 times; on the final repeat, omit the last bobble; instead, sl st in the top loops of the ch-1 following the beginning bobble— 15 bobbles, 5 ch-5 sps.

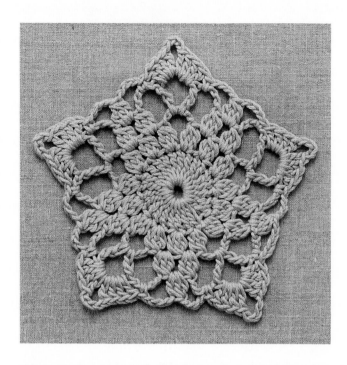

CONSTELLATION MINOR PENT

CONSTELLATION MAJOR PENT

RND 3: Ch 2, dc2tog in the beginning ch-1 sp *(this equals a beginning bobble)*; *ch 1, make a bobble in the next ch-1 sp; ch 4, (tr, ch 4, tr) in the next ch-5 sp; ch 4, make a bobble in the next ch-1 sp*; repeat from * to * 4 times; on the final repeat, omit the last bobble; instead, sl st in the top loops of the ch-1 following the beginning bobble.

Constellation Minor Pent: Last Round

RND 4: Ch 2, dc2tog in the beginning ch-1 sp *(this equals a beginning bobble)*; *ch 4 (or join), sc in the next ch-4 sp; *(no ch 4 here)* [4 dc, ch 4 (or join), 4 dc] in the next ch-4 sp; *(no ch 4 here)* sc in the next ch-4 sp; ch 4 (or join), make a bobble in the next ch-1 sp*; repeat from * to * 4 times; on the final repeat, omit the last bobble, instead, sl st in the top loops of the ch-1 following the beginning bobble. Fasten off.

Constellation Major Pent: Last Rounds

RND 4: Ch 2, dc2tog in the beginning ch-1 sp *(this equals a beginning bobble)*; *ch 4, sc in the next ch-4 sp; ch 4, [sc, ch 4, sc] in the next ch-4 sp; ch 4, sc in the next ch-4 sp**; ch 4, make a bobble in the next ch-1 sp*; repeat from * to * 3 times, then repeat from * to **; ch 1, dc in the top loops of the ch-1 following the beginning bobble *(this equals ch 4)*—25 ch-4 sps.

RND 5: Ch 1, sc in the beginning sp; *[ch 4 (or join), sc in the next ch-4 sp] 2 times; *(no ch 4 here)* [4 dc, (ch 4 or join), 4 dc] in the next ch-4 sp; *(no ch 4 here)* sc in the next ch-4 sp; ch 4 (or join), sc in the next ch-4 sp*; repeat from * to * 4 times; on the final repeat, omit the last sc; instead, sl st in the beginning sc. Fasten off.

CONSTELLATION HEXES: CENTER ROUNDS

Ch 4; sl st in the beginning ch to form a ring.

RND 1: Ch 1, sc in the ring; [ch 3, sc in the ring] 5 times; dc in the beginning sc (*this equals ch 3*)—6 ch-3 sps.

RND 2: Ch 4 (*this equals tr*), 4 tr in the first ch-3 sp; 5 tr in each of the next 5 ch-3 sps; sl st in the 4th ch of the beginning ch—30 tr.

RND 3: Ch 2, dc2tog in the first tr (*this equals a beginning bobble*); *[ch 1, skip the next tr, make a bobble in the next tr] 2 times; ch 5, (*do not skip here*) make a bobble in the next stitch*; repeat from * to * 5 times; on the final repeat, omit the last bobble; instead, sl st in the top loops of the ch-1 following the beginning bobble.

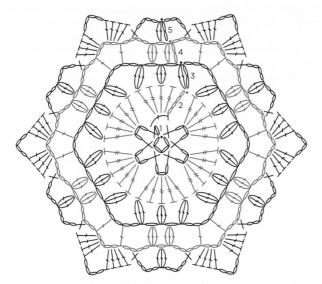

CONSTELLATION MINOR HEX

CONSTELLATION MAJOR HEX

RND 4: Ch 2, dc2tog in the beginning ch-1 sp (*this equals a beginning bobble*); *ch 1, make a bobble in the next ch-1 sp; ch 4, [dc, ch 4, dc] in the next ch-5 sp; ch 4, make a bobble in the next ch-1 sp*; repeat from * to * 5 times; on the final repeat, omit the last bobble; instead, sl st in the top loops of the ch-1 following the beginning bobble.

Constellation Minor Hex: Last Round

RND 5: Ch 2, dc2tog in the beginning ch-1 sp (*this equals a beginning bobble*); *ch 4 (or join), sc in the next ch-4 sp; (*no ch 4 here*) [4 dc, ch 4 (or join), 4 dc] in the next ch-4 sp; (*no ch 4 here*) sc in the next ch-4 sp; ch 4 (or join), make a bobble in the next ch-1 sp*; repeat from * to * 5 times; on the final repeat, omit the last bobble; instead, sl st in the top loops of the ch-1 following the beginning bobble. Fasten off.

Constellation Major Hex: Last Rounds

RND 5: Ch 2, dc2tog in the beginning ch-1 sp (*this equals a beginning bobble*); *ch 4, sc in the next ch-4 sp; ch 4, (sc, ch 4, sc) in the next ch-4 sp; ch 4, sc in the next ch-4 sp**; ch 4, make a bobble in the next ch-1 sp*; repeat from * to * 4 times, then repeat from * to **; ch 1, dc in the top loops of the ch-1 following the beginning bobble.

RND 6: Ch 1, sc in the beginning sp; *[ch 4 (or join), sc in the next ch-4 sp] 2 times; (*no ch 4 here*) [4 dc, ch 4 (or join), 4 dc] in the next ch-4 sp; (*no ch 4 here*) sc in the next ch-4 sp; ch 4 (or join), sc in the next ch-4 sp*; repeat from * to * 5 times; on the final repeat, omit the last sc; instead, sl st in the beginning sc. Fasten off.

CONSTELLATION MINOR OCT

CONSTELLATION MAJOR OCT

CONSTELLATION OCTS: CENTER ROUNDS

Ch 4; sl st in the first ch to form a ring.

RND 1: Ch 3 *(this equals dc)*; 15 dc in the ring; sl st in the 3rd ch of the beginning ch—16 dc.

RND 2: Ch 1, sc in the first dc; [ch 3, skip the next dc, sc in the next dc] 7 times; dc in the beginning sc *(this equals ch 3)*—8 ch-3 sps.

RND 3: Ch 4 *(this equals tr)*, 4 tr in the first ch-3 sp; 5 tr in each of the next 7 ch-3 sps; sl st in the 4th ch of the beginning ch—40 tr.

RND 4: Ch 2, dc2tog in the first tr *(this equals a beginning bobble)*; *[ch 1, skip the next tr, make a bobble in the next tr] 2 times; ch 5, *(do not skip here)* make a bobble in the next tr*; repeat from * to * 7 times; on the final repeat,

omit the last bobble; instead, sl st in the top loops of the ch-1 following the beginning bobble—24 bobbles, 8 ch-5 sps.

RND 5: Ch 2, dc2tog in the beginning ch-1 sp *(this equals a beginning bobble)*; *ch 1, make a bobble in the next ch-1 sp; ch 4, [dc, ch 4, dc] in the next ch-5 sp; ch 4, make a bobble in the next ch-1 sp*; repeat from * to * 7 times; on the final repeat, omit the last bobble; instead, sl st in the top loops of the ch-1 following the beginning bobble.

Constellation Minor Oct: Last Round

RND 6: Ch 2, dc2tog in the beginning ch-1 sp *(this equals a beginning bobble)*; *ch 4 (or join), sc in the next ch-4 sp; (no ch 4 here)* [4 dc, ch 4 (or join), 4 dc] in the next ch-4 sp; *(no ch 4 here)* sc in the next ch-4 sp; ch 4 (or join), make a bobble in the next ch-1 sp*; repeat from * to * 7 times; on the final repeat, omit the last bobble; instead, sl st in the top loops of the ch-1 that closes the beginning bobble. Fasten off.

Constellation Major Oct: Last Rounds

RND 6: Ch 2, dc2tog in the beginning ch-1 sp *(this equals a beginning bobble)*; *ch 4, sc in the next ch-4 sp; ch 4, (sc, ch 4, sc) in the next ch-4 sp; ch 4, sc in the next ch-4 sp**; ch 4, make a bobble in the next ch-1 sp*; repeat from * to * 6 times, then repeat from * to **; ch 1, dc in the top loops of the ch-1 following the beginning bobble *(this equals ch 4)*.

RND 7: Ch 1, sc in the beginning sp; *[ch 4 (or join), sc in the next ch-4 sp] 2 times; *(no ch 4 here)* [4 dc, ch 4 (or join), 4 dc] in the next ch-4 sp; *(no ch 4 here)*, sc in the next ch-4 sp; ch 4 (or join), sc in the next ch-4 sp*; repeat from * to * 7 times; on the final repeat, omit the last sc; instead, sl st in the beginning sc. Fasten off.

Universal Assembly

Motifs are the building blocks that will be crocheted together into garment shapes according to assembly diagrams. The pattern text will not always give stitch-by-stitch crochet instructions about connecting the motifs to one another. Rather, you should become familiar with the general joining techniques described in this section.

WHAT'S THIS MAJOR/MINOR THING?

Every motif in this book is completed with a last round of ch-4 spaces: there is a ch-4 sp at each of the polygon points and either two (for all minor class motifs) or three (for all major class motifs) at each polygon side. This is huge. It allows for the assembly of any motifs within a class and opens the door to swapping styles of motifs in a design. In other words, because the outer rounds of all minor class motifs are essentially the same, they can all be connected to one another no matter what the style or configuration. The same is true for all major class motifs.

DO I HAVE TO FOLLOW THE ASSEMBLY DIAGRAM?

For a few of the projects the order of assembly is not critical, and you are free to put the motifs together however you please. But for the complex garments there are numbered motifs with detailed text to go with the diagrams. I've tried to make the pieces of a design come together in the way you'd probably want to do it. If you can bring yourself to stick to the program and follow the assembly text and diagrams to the letter, then you have every hope for success.

The polygons represented in the assembly diagrams look strange and misshapen. To a certain extent the actual motifs as crocheted in a project will also end up looking a little wonky. No worries. This is part of the plan. We are relying on the shape-shifting properties of the parts. This is yarn, not steel, brick, and mortar. That's what makes the unusual, counterintuitive assemblies possible. The lace, particularly the motif points, will bend, stretch, and adjust as required.

Why, yes, you can wander off the page and put these motifs together to make stuff other than the designs in this book—the more outside the box, the better.

HOW DO I MAKE A JOIN?

All motifs are connected to one another as you go, while crocheting the last round. Begin by crocheting the motif up to the last round, then begin the last round and stop just before the ch-4 sp of a point. Connections go from the ch-sp of a point, across the ch-sps of a side, to the ch-sp of the next point.

With the right side facing, hold the working motif (the one being completed) alongside the previous motif (the one already assembled into the fabric). I find it easier to have the working motif to the left (my nonhook hand) and the previous motif to the right (my hook hand).

Join: Wherever you need to make a connection, replace the ch-4 sp of the last round with: [ch 2, sl st from front to back in the corresponding ch-4 sp of the previous motif, ch 2].

Join at a side space: After making the indicated stitch at the side of the working motif, ch 2, insert the hook from front to back in the next ch-4 sp of the motif to which you are making the connection, and sl st, ch 2. Then return to make the next stitch of the working motif.

Join in an unpopulated point space: After making the first 4 dc at a point of the working motif, ch 2, insert the hook from front to back in the point ch-4 sp of the motif to which you are making the connection, sl st, ch 2, and complete the point of the working motif with 4 dc in the same sp. Then sc in the next ch-4 sp of the working motif.

Join another point in an existing join: Where there is already one join at a point, make the slip stitch in the slip stitch of the existing join under two strands. This is critical. This ensures that the completed point joins are stable, compact, and most attractive, and yet still allows for the whole join to move and adjust.

WHERE DO I FIND THE SINGULARITY?

That sweet spot, the stable place in an existing slip stitch join, the two strands of a join that I prefer for the singularity is not the easiest thing to locate. You might have to dig for it by stretching the points in opposite directions to make the loops of the slip stitch join pull away from the ch-4 sp to which it is joined. You should now see four strands between the top loops of the slip stitch and the ch-4 sp.

These strands, two at the right side or front of the work and two at the wrong side or back of the work, wrap around the ch-4 sp, cradle it, and ride freely along it. Insert the hook between the two strands at the front AND between the two strands at the back, avoiding the top loops of the sl st and the chains of the previous ch-4 sp.

Technically, you are inserting the hook not into the slip stitch itself but into two strands of the next chain beyond the top loops of the slip stitch. Told you it would be complicated! Make any subsequent join at that singularity by inserting the hook into that same place.

FIRST MAJOR MOTIF

JOINING MAJOR MOTIF
ON TWO SIDES

FIRST MINOR MOTIF

JOINING MAJOR MOTIF
ON ONE SIDE

JOINING MINOR MOTIF
ON TWO SIDES

Here are hypothetical examples of joins among three minor hex motifs and among three major hex motifs.

JOINING MINOR MOTIF
ON ONE SIDE

Measuring Motifs

Every design using motifs lists the target measurements in the Gauge section at the beginning of each pattern. Here's what the numbers are measuring:

In addition to measurements for the completed whole motifs, there will be at least one checkpoint at an earlier round. Do the checkpoint measurement to see if you are in close enough orbit. If your checkpoint gauge is way off, start over by crocheting looser or tighter as needed, perhaps with a different size hook or a different thickness yarn. If you are on target or nearly correct, then go ahead and make the whole motif and compare it to the stated finished measurements.

To measure, either at a checkpoint or after a last round, stretch the motif in all directions, smooth it out, but let it snap back if it wants to. I like to use a clear plastic ruler for measuring crochet. Measure from edge to edge, including all yarn, whatever is there. Take measurements from more than one side, diameter, angle to double-check the results.

Since the motifs are joined to each other as you go, you will hardly ever see a whole, unattached motif during the process of crocheting a project. The moment motifs are locked into fabric, their measurements will always shift and adjust to serve the needs of the garment shape, so you might not get accurate whole measurements of assembled motifs. Take the opportunity to do a checkpoint measurement for each motif as you make it to help you stay on track.

If you are working with a yarn that is unfamiliar and you don't know how it will perform for you, then you might want to make tests of each of the different motifs required in the design, complete but unassembled. Once you get them to the stated gauge, keep them around for reference.

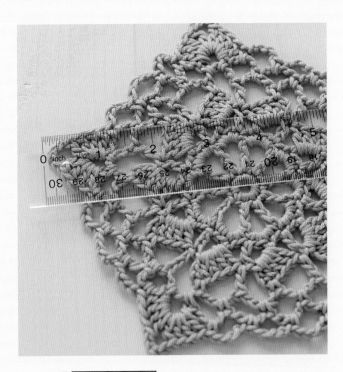

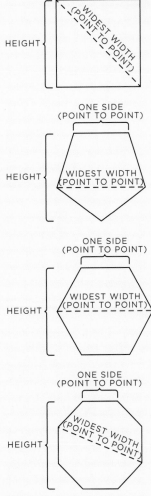

Working with Motifs

FASTENING OFF

Every motif here ends with a slip stitch in the beginning stitch of the last round. The slip stitch does not count as anything. To fasten off, pull up the last loop on the hook a couple of inches. Cut the feeder yarn, then pull the cut tail all the way through.

GENEROUS TAILS

Leave enough yarn in the tails, both at the beginning of the motif center and at the end when you fasten off. You'll want enough remaining length for threading onto a tapestry needle and weaving in the ends.

WEAVING ENDS

Weave in the loose ends every now and then. A good time to police your ends is after completing a course of motifs. If you keep up with end weaving you'll have fewer annoying strands in the way while you are working and less of a chore when you're done. By weaving I mean thread each tail on the finest tapestry needle you can manage and sew it up and down, back and forth on the wrong side, hiding your sewing inside the stitches of the work.

WEAVING THE BEGINNING TAIL

Yes, you should weave it, even if you habitually loop the beginning tail around the center of the motif and work over it while crocheting the first round. With loose gauge lace, merely crocheting over the end is not secure enough to keep it from worming out. Thread the end on a tapestry needle and sew into the motif center at least once all the way around, hiding the weaving under the stems of the first round of stitches.

FIXING SLOPPY CENTER HOLES

Chances are the holes at the centers of same configuration motifs aren't all the same size. If you're an obsessive freak like me when it comes to consistency, then please take this opportunity to even them up while weaving in the beginning tail. Give the tail a tug to tighten up a sloppy hole before weaving it securely into the motif center.

Why not use the so-called Magic Loop technique for the beginning ring of motifs? I never write the Magic Loop in published patterns because I can't be sure that the yarn you want to use will survive the process. Magic Loop depends on the ability of one strand of yarn to withstand the tugging that is required to tighten the loop and the pressure of holding the entire motif at the center. Most of the yarns here are either not smooth enough or not sturdy enough. See stress test (page 138; see "Crocheted Buttons"). If your yarn passes, then use Magic Loop at your discretion. Since the loop has no knot or anchor, a tail that is not thoroughly woven in will come loose if you breathe on it. You must weave the beginning end securely or risk releasing the loop.

BINDING MOTIF EDGES

Motif edges are forced to be purposeful and restrained when they are connected to others in an assembly. They do their jobs. But unattached motif edges will expand and stretch as much as they can get away with. You can take advantage of this expansive nature for added ease or a bit of flare to the hem of a skirt or to armholes by leaving the edges as they are, unbound.

But to control unruly motif edges or to continue with headers, bands, and ribbing, they need to be bound. There are two techniques for binding motif edges used here. One is to create a foundation strip that is then assembled to the motif edge with a connecting round. The other is to crochet a row or round of chain spaces directly to the motif edge, which may then be worked with stitches to continue for a band or ribbing. The patterns will give instructions for the specific binding used in each garment. But following are general examples, FYI.

BINDING WITH A FOUNDATION

The bound edge can be as loose or as relaxed as needed by juggling the length of the foundation and the number of stitches you take up as you connect each motif. Minor class motifs have one less ch-sp in a side than their sister major class motifs. But by using a relaxed connecting round and a controlled connecting round respectively, both classes of motif can be bound to the same number of foundation stitches. Opposite are hypothetical examples of the two types, both using 20 foundation dc for each motif side.

DIRECT BINDING

The ribbed waistband of Titan (page 75) and the body band of the Phoebe Shrug (page 93) use the direct application technique. See page 78 for diagrams of this technique as used on minor and major class motif edges.

SIZING WITH MOTIFS

The best outcome when designing sizes is for everyone to have exactly the same garment drape while maintaining proper body proportions, using the same yarn, hook, and gauge so that each size gets the same fabric. A few of the patterns in this book, the skirts in particular (Tempest, page 16, and Galaxy, page 71), generate extra sizing by adjusting the number of pattern repeats and motifs around the body so the skirts are pretty much the same fabric across the range.

But there are difficulties in sizing motif constructions that require specific geometry in order for the parts to fit together. You can't change the numbers of motifs, but to a limited extent you can change the number of rounds in the motifs. That's what the classes

Minor and Major are about. For every Minor motif there is a Major version containing an extra round. Sizing can be accomplished by swapping out a Minor for a Major and vice versa. However, that isn't enough to create more than two different sizes for motif garments. So we go to Plan B.

PLAN B: SIZING WITH GAUGE

You can see examples of gauge-executed sizing in the designs Kerry Top (page 121) and Andromeda (page 126), where the third size requires a set of extended gauge motifs in the same design yarn but crocheted with a larger hook. Trust me, it was incredibly difficult to predict what would happen to the garment proportions when using looser motifs.

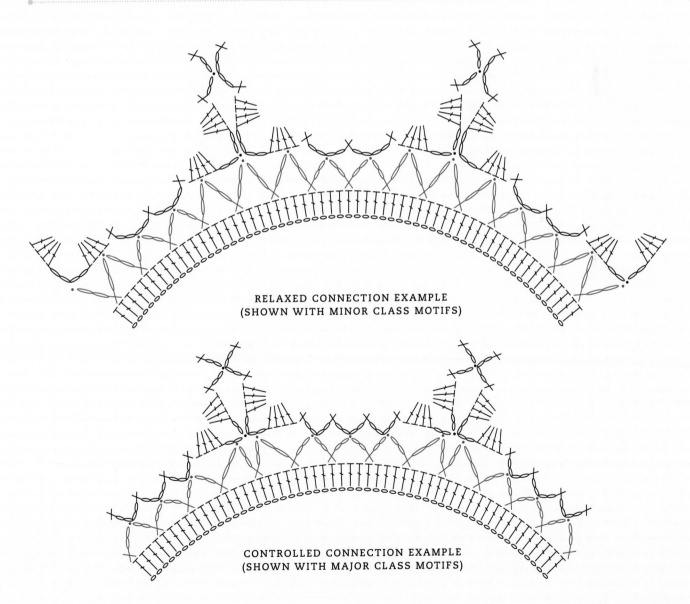

RELAXED CONNECTION EXAMPLE
(SHOWN WITH MINOR CLASS MOTIFS)

CONTROLLED CONNECTION EXAMPLE
(SHOWN WITH MAJOR CLASS MOTIFS)

Sizing by altering the gauge means changing the size of every single stitch you crochet, accurately and consistently. This requires you to (1) understand how I—the designer and sample maker—crochet; (2) understand how you crochet; (3) know how to crochet a different gauge and maintain it throughout an entire project; (4) calculate a target gauge that won't be given in the instructions; and (5) be prepared for a garment that doesn't look, drape, or fit exactly like the sample I made for photography. Scary, huh? That said, there are a few things you can control in order to purposefully alter gauge.

What Changes Gauge: Intentional Tension, Hook, Yarn

Intentional tension is when you change the way in which you crochet. By making your hands do the work more tightly or loosely it is possible to create garments that are larger or smaller than offered in the pattern. This can be very hard to do because you are fighting your normal habits and inclinations. This can be as simple as wrapping the feeder one more time around your fingers, lifting or not lifting up on your stitches each time, or working slowly and deliberately with thought.

Changing hooks often does the trick. Every pattern gives a recommended hook size, followed by the suggestion "or size needed to obtain gauge," meaning that you are encouraged, even expected, to switch hooks until you get the stated gauge. In the same way you can purposefully target a smaller or larger gauge by using a smaller or larger hook. Consider also changing the hook style or material.

Swapping yarn will always change gauge. For example, if the garment is designed in DK or light worsted weight yarn and you want to make a size larger than offered in the pattern, you could bump the gauge by using full worsted yarn. Even if you use the same size hook as written, your gauge is sure to be bigger, although it's usually better to match thicker yarn with a larger hook, too. Sometimes all that's needed is a different type or fiber yarn. Say the design is created with a DK wool yarn. By switching to a DK cotton or alpaca or acrylic yarn you could have enough of a gauge difference to make another size.

What, Me? Calculate?

Look at the images and the schematic for the design you want to resize. See how the motifs contribute to each measurement of the garment. Most of the tops in this book use six motifs side-to-side or point-to-point around the bust, the neckline, and the waist. Do a bit of addition or subtraction and multiply by six. Extrapolate what will happen if you change the dimensions of all the parts. I do this every time I size a design. You can, too.

It doesn't take a huge change in the dimensions of a motif in order to get a few inches in extra garment size. Each small jump in one piece of the puzzle will be multiplied over many pieces. Think in terms of motifs that are a fraction of an inch smaller or larger at the widest point-to-point measurement stated.

Remember that sizing with gauge will change everything: every proportion, circumference, length, and depth. Take a look at Zodiac (page 81) compared to Callisto (page 87). These two tops share the same motif assembly, with an octagon at the center of the body ringed by pentagons. See how the DK gauge Zodiac is an oversize tunic. See how the fine gauge Callisto is a teeny waist-cropped vest. These represent extremes, but serve to illustrate the contrast between big and small motif gauges using the same construction.

If taken too far your result may no longer have human proportions. Zodiac in worsted gauge would certainly be roomier in the bust but might come to your knees. Zodiac in sportweight might have a slimmer profile in the body but will have sleeves that are too small to go around your arms. Callisto in superfine gauge might not cover your bust. Just saying.

Motif edges are kept purposeful and restrained when they are connected to others in an assembly. They do their jobs. But unattached motif edges will expand and stretch as much as they can get away with. Know that you can fix an overly loose neckline, armhole, or lower edge by adding a bound edge to control the extra fullness if there isn't one in the design. Do not hesitate to work any bands tighter or looser as needed to get the opening size you want.

Be prepared to make lots of test motifs. Make a test of each of the configuration motifs (square, pent, hex, or oct) and check the gauge of all. Go through whatever changes you need, using different tensions, hooks, and yarns, until you're happy not just with the measurements of the motif, but with the look and feel of them. I don't want you to proceed to make a garment if your motifs are so dense that they have zero stretch or drape, nor do I want to see you using motifs that are falling apart. These designs depend on the ability of the lace to shift around and play the part that's needed. If you go too far with gauge, you could change the way the motifs behave when assembled.

Mine Doesn't Look the Same

And it never will. There is no avoiding the fact that changing the gauge will create differences in fabric, fit, and proportions for smaller or larger than written sizes. That's kind of the point. What you create is yours and meant to fit your body. Don't worry about comparing it to the samples.

Tweaking gauge is not just for sizing whole garments. Who says you must work the same gauge all over? You have the tools to fine-tune the fit of anything you make, targeting adjustments to the area you need, whether or not you are resizing. For example, the Andromeda Dress (page 131) is a proportionally slimmer fit through the hip. You could crochet the skirt motifs in a slightly looser gauge and create extra ease. I did something similar when I was presented with models who were very different sizes (see photo at left). The model on the right in the Andromeda Dress is a slim size 4 and the XS/S sample dress fit a bit loose on her, so we used a belt to create a draped, blouson effect. However, the model on the left in the mustard-colored Andromeda Pepulm Vest is a curvier size 8. To give her more ease at the bottom I worked the waist finishing, the header, and the entire peplum in a slightly looser gauge, and it draped exceptionally well over her more generous hips.

INSIDE THE BOX:
squares

It's easy to dismiss the utilitarian square as just another brick in the wall. Your early experience with motif crochet probably began as did mine with the traditional "granny square." From my mother I learned invaluable lessons from those first square projects about working crochet in the round, grokking the mysteries of corners, and securing ends so they don't come back to embarrass you later. But, dense as bricks held together with the mortar of crocheted or sewn seams using additional yarn, those early objects were essentially rows and columns of . . . pot holders.

I now know better. Made in relaxed gauges and joined as you go, traditional grannies can be very happy. But a total love affair developed when I stumbled onto stitch guides and vintage thread patterns featuring lace squares. My early lessons served me well as I began translating these intricate lace motif doilies, bedspreads, and antimacassars into exploded gauge garments. Although they're still squares assembled in straight rows and columns, the results don't have to be rigidly boxy. I say let the "cromance" begin.

telesto STOLE

Light and soft as a whisper, but with lovely impact, Telesto is an example of how exploded gauge squares can be visually interesting as well as delightful to wear. The luxury yarn and unexpected bold color lift this simple rectangle beyond the sum of its thirty-six square parts.

skill level

EASY   ● ○ ○

Size

60" (152.5cm) long by 15" (38cm) wide

Materials

Filatura Di Crosa Superior; 70% cashmere, 25% schappe silk, 5% extrafine merino; ⅞ oz (25g), 330 yd (300m) **1** Super Fine

2 balls in #53 Cobalt, or approximately 610 yd (667m) fingering weight yarn

U.S. Size 7 (4.5mm) crochet hook or size needed to obtain gauge

Gauge

Carina or Constellation Minor Square Motif

One side, point to point = 5" (12.5cm)

NOTE: *If you mix and match styles of squares you may need to use slightly tighter or looser tension for each of the different centers in order for the* finished diameters to all be the same. Gauge is not critical for this rectangle, except for yarn usage. If your square motifs are a bit smaller or larger than 5"(12.5cm), no worries. You may simply stop crocheting when you're satisfied with the length of the stole . . . or when you run out of yarn. I had a few grams left over from two balls of this gorgeous but fairly expensive yarn, which will provide enough leeway yardage for this project as written, even if your gauge is a little off.

Stitch Definitions

See instructions for individual Carina minor square motifs (page 25) and Constellation minor square motifs (page 29).

For more motif assembly information, see Universal Assembly (page 33).

Instructions

Telesto uses two different motif styles in an alternating checkerboard array. You may use any of the squares I've offered in Spawn of Entropy or make all 36 squares the same, or use more than one color. I prefer assembling across the short 3-motif width first, then building on with successive rows of 3 motifs. This works well in case you run out of yarn and need to make fewer motifs or you prefer a longer stole, as you can easily omit or add a row of 3 to alter the length without undue deconstruction.

MOTIFS 1–36: Make 18 Carina minor squares and 18 Constellation minor squares, connecting them completely to one another as you go while working the last round according to the assembly diagram.

Weave in the ends. Wet block the stole (BFF, page 142) and gently smooth the stole to the finished dimensions.

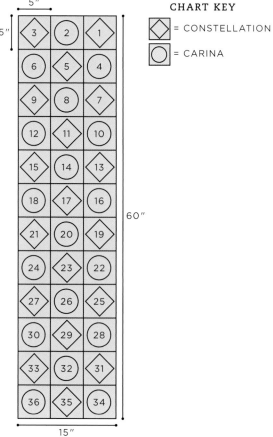

CHART KEY

◇ = CONSTELLATION

◯ = CARINA

gliese COWL

Although this pretty wrap is constructed with squares in rows and columns, it is anything but flat. By giving one end of a rectangle a half twist before seamlessly connecting to the other end, you can create a continuous mobius or infinity loop that drapes artfully as it embraces the shoulders or frames the face.

Size

42″ (106.5cm) long by 18″ (45.5cm) deep rectangle, half-twisted and connected into a mobius

Materials

Prism Yarns Windward Layers; 63% rayon, 37% cotton; 4 oz (113g)/200 yd (183m) Medium

3 hanks in Prairie, or approximately 550 yd (600m) light worsted weight yarn

U.S. Size I-9 (5.5mm) crochet hook or size needed to obtain gauge

Gauge

Copernicus Minor Square Motif

RND 2: 2½″ (6.4cm) diameter

RND 4: 5¼″ (13cm) widest

RND 5: one side, point to point = 6″ (15.2cm)

Stitch Definitions

See instructions for individual Copernicus minor square motifs (page 22).

For more motif assembly information, see Universal Assembly (page 33).

Instructions

Gliese is made of 21 squares assembled into a rectangle, with one end given a half twist before connecting the rectangle into a continuous mobius cowl.

MOTIFS 1–18: Make 18 Copernicus minor square motifs, connecting them completely to one another as you go while working the last round according to the assembly diagram.

The last 3 motifs are connected to one another and to both short edges of the rectangle. With the right side of the rectangle facing, flip the bottom edge (Motifs 16, 17, 18) over to the wrong side and bring the top and bottom edges close together, matching the end of Motif 1 with Motif 18, Motif 2 with Motif 17, and Motif 3 with Motif 16.

NOTE: *It doesn't matter in which order the last 3 motifs are added, nor does it matter which end of the rectangle is right- or wrong-side-facing. For the diagram I have specified which goes where.*

MOTIF 19: Connect from the first point to the second point to the wrong-side-facing edge of Motif 18, then connect from the third point to the fourth point to the right-side-facing edge of Motif 1. Finish the rest of the motif.

MOTIF 20: Connect completely to Motif 2, Motif 19, and to the wrong-side-facing edge of Motif 17. Finish the rest of the motif.

MOTIF 21: Connect completely to Motif 3, Motif 20, and to the wrong-side-facing edge of Motif 16. Finish the rest of the motif.

Weave in the ends. Block the cowl as best as you can, smoothing the lace into the twisted shape as shown in the schematic.

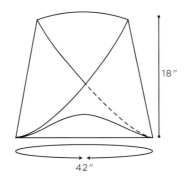

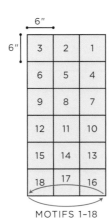

MOTIFS 1–18

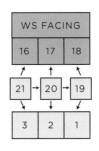

skyliner
SKIRT AND PONCHO

With a sensual shapeliness that belies its square origin, Skyliner proves that it's hot to be square. This time the rectangle is connected end-to-side to form a cone shape. With an added drawstring band (a header) Skyliner is as at home in high, close orbit around the shoulders poncho-style as it is slung around the hips as an asymmetric-hem skirt.

skill level
INTERMEDIATE ● ● ○

Size

S/M (L/XL, Plus), sample shown is size S/M

Finished waist/neck 32 (36½, 41)", (81 [92.5, 104]cm); length at straight side 20" (51cm); length at diagonal point 27½" (70cm); circumference, bottom 67½ (72, 76½)" (171.5 [183, 194.5]cm)

FIT TIP: *Size S/M will fit most as a poncho and is the best choice for this. Sizes L/XL and Plus have a larger top opening, which will allow the piece to fit over a more generous waist and hips as a skirt, but this could make a slightly awkward poncho because of the extra fabric around the neck.*

Materials

Louisa Harding Mulberry; 100% silk; 1¾ oz (50g), 136 yd (124m) (3) Light

6 (7, 7) skeins in #34 Rouge, or approximately 750 (830, 890) yd (686 [759, 814]m) DK or sport weight yarn

U.S. Size 7 (4.5mm) crochet hook or size needed to obtain gauge

Gauge

14 fsc = 4" (10cm)

Carina Minor Square Motif

RND 2: 2½" (6.3cm)

RND 5: one side, point to point = 4½" (11.5cm); widest diagonal = 6⅓" (16 cm)

Stitch Definitions

FSC (FOUNDATION SINGLE CROCHET): See Chainless Foundations (page 140).

See instructions for individual Carina minor square motifs (page 25).

For more motif assembly information, see Universal Assembly (page 33).

Instructions

Skyliner is made of 44 (48, 52) squares assembled into a rectangle, with one short side connected to part of one long side to form a cone shape.

MOTIFS 1–40 (44, 48): Make 40 (44, 48) Carina minor square motifs, connecting them completely to one another as you go while working the last round according to the assembly diagram.

The last 4 motifs are connected to one another, to one short edge of the rectangle, and to the sides of 4 motifs along a long edge. With the right side of the rectangle facing, curve the bottom edge around, bringing the last row of 4 motifs close to the long edge, matching the ends to Motifs 1, 5, 9, and 13.

MOTIF 41 (45, 49): Connect from the first point to the second point to the edge of Motif 37 (41, 45), then connect from the third point to the fourth point to the edge of Motif 1. Finish the rest of the motif.

MOTIF 42 (46, 50): Connect completely to Motif 38 (42, 46), to Motif 41 (45, 49), and to Motif 5. Finish the rest of the motif.

MOTIF 43 (47, 51): Connect completely to Motif 39 (43, 47), to Motif 42 (46, 50), and to Motif 9. Finish the rest of the motif.

MOTIF 44 (48, 52): Connect completely to Motif 40 (44, 48), to Motif 43 (47, 51), and to Motif 13. Finish the rest of the motif.

Weave in the ends.

Waist/Neck Finishing

Skyliner has a bound waist/neckline with a header (for more information, see Binding Motif Edges, page 36) that creates spaces for threading the string.

Fsc 112 (128, 144) to measure approximately 32 (36½, 41)" (81 [92.5, 104]cm). *(To measure, stretch the foundation, let it snap back if it wants to, and then measure from end to end.)* Bring the ends of the foundation together, being careful not to twist the stitches, and sl st in the beginning stitch to form a ring. Begin work across the sc edge of the foundation.

With the right side of the waist/neck edge *(the smaller opening of the cone)* facing, hold the foundation ring to the nonhook side and the motif edge on the hook side. Bouncing back and forth, as you would to connect motif sides, connect the foundation to the 7 (8,

9) motif sides of the waist/neck edge, using 16 foundation stitches per motif side. Begin with the first connection in any partial chain space just past the join between motifs.

TIP: *Just before closing the following Connecting Rnd, bring the feeder yarn to the wrong side of the work so it is in the proper place to continue the header.*

CONNECTING RND (RS): Ch 1, sc in the first sc of the foundation; *ch 2, sl st in the next partial ch-sp of the motif; ch 2, skip the next 3 sc of the foundation, sc in the next sc; [ch 2, sl st in the next ch-4 sp of the motif; ch 2, skip the next 3 sc of the foundation, sc in the next sc] 2 times; ch 2, sl st in the next partial ch-sp of the motif, ch 2, skip the next 3 sc of the foundation, sc in the next sc*; repeat from * to * 6 (7, 8) times; on the final repeat, omit the last sc; instead, sl st in the beginning sc of the round. Continue with the header—28 (32, 36) ch-sp joins.

Header

Rotate so the chain edge of the foundation is on top (move the feeder yarn now to the wrong side, the inside of the body). Sl st in the stem of the beginning sc of the Connecting Rnd (the one just joined in); sl st in the chain of the foundation just above. Reach across the gap and sl st in the last ch of the foundation. Begin to work around the chain edge.

TIP: *The foundation for sizes S/M and L/XL is not in a multiple of 3. For the nicest header, you will want to end with an even number of hdc Vs. For size S/M, squeeze in an added V by skipping just one ch before a V at two places evenly spaced along the header; for size L/XL, use up the extra 2 foundation stitches by skipping three chs before a V at two places evenly spaced along the header.*

HEADER RND 1 (RS): Ch 4 (*this equals hdc, ch 2*), hdc in the same foundation ch stitch; [skip the next 2 chains, (hdc, ch 2, hdc) in the next ch] around; skip the last 2 chains, sl st in the 2nd ch of the beginning ch—38 (42, 48) ch-2 sps.

HEADER RND 2 (RS): Ch 1, 3 sc in each ch-2 sp around; sl st in the beginning sc. Fasten off—114 (126, 144) sc.

Weave in the ends, and block.

String

Skyliner requires a drawstring. Choose a string type (page 137) as desired, and make one string 44 (48, 53)" (112 [122, 134.5]cm) long or to taste. Weave the string in and out of the spaces between the Vs of the hdc stitches in the header, centering the ends of the string at the notch of the V.

MOTIFS 1–40 (44, 48)

4	3	2	1
8	7	6	5
12	11	10	9
16	15	14	13
20	19	18	17
24	23	22	21
28	27	26	25
32	31	30	29
36	35	34	33
40	39	38	37

S/M

| 44 | 43 | 42 | 41 |

L/XL

| 48 | 47 | 46 | 45 |

PLUS

TO JOIN LAST ROW
OF EACH SIZE, REFER
TO INSETS ON THE SIDE

17	13	9	5	1
49 →	50 →	51 →	52
45	46	47	48

JOINING OF LAST 4 MOTIFS
SIZE PLUS

17	13	9	5	1
45 ‹	46 →	47 →	48
44	43	42	41

JOINING OF LAST 4 MOTIFS
SIZE L/XL

17	13	9	5	1
44 →	43 →	42 →	41
40	39	38	37

JOINING OF LAST 4 MOTIFS
SIZE S/M

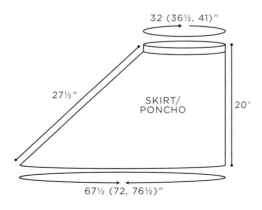

32 (36½, 41)"

27½"

SKIRT/
PONCHO

20'

67½ (72, 76½)"

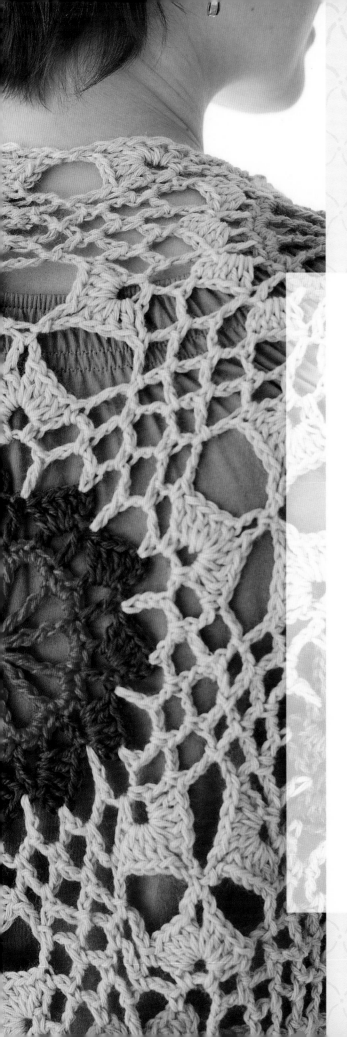

HEY NINETEEN:
hexagons

Plane geometry dictates that there can be many combinations of polygons that will tile, or fit together flat leaving no spaces; very few polygons will tile when used alone. Squares, those gems with perfect ninety-degree angles at each of the four corners, are tiling fools. Feel free to play with a variety of square configurations, assembling in rows and columns for lacy scarves, stoles, and throws.

More interesting are hexes, which have more personality. The outer edges of hexagon arrays are not straight and neat. These huge scallops and bumps can create interesting objects. And in an exploded gauge, it doesn't take very many hexes to make something happen. Here are a few possibilities for using tiled hexagonal motifs in arrays of just nineteen (or eighteen . . . or twenty).

carina

SHAWL AND THROW

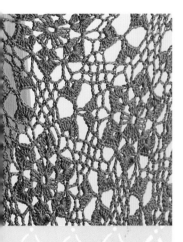

You'll love how pleasantly and quickly this pretty lace motif throw comes together. It's a basic hexagon composed of, hey, nineteen hexagons.

skill level

EASY ● ○ ○

Size

48" (122cm) diameter at widest point

Materials

Caron International Simply Soft, 100% acrylic, 6 oz (170g), 315 yd (288m) **④** Medium

3 skeins in 0010 Cypress, or approximately 900 yd (823m) worsted weight yarn

U.S. Size J-10 (6mm) crochet hook or size needed to obtain gauge

Gauge

Carina Major Hex Motif

RND 1: 3" (7.5cm) diameter

RND 2: 4½" (11.5cm) diameter

RND 6: one side, point to point = 6" (15cm); height = 9½" (24cm); widest point = 11" (28cm)

Please see Measuring Motifs (page 35).

Stitch Definitions

See instructions for individual Carina major hex motifs (page 27).

For more motif assembly information, see Universal Assembly (page 33).

Instructions

MOTIFS 1–19: Make 19 Carina hex motifs, connecting them completely to one another as you go while working the last round according to the assembly diagram.

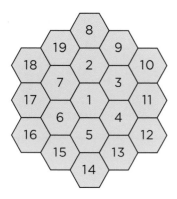

Here are three alternate assemblies for nice-sized projects that feature tiled hex motifs in worsted weight gauge. Any of the major hex motifs will work, so feel free to swap them out.

This 19-motif array makes a generous rectangular-ish stole or throw, approximately 66″ (168cm) long and 28″ (71cm) wide.

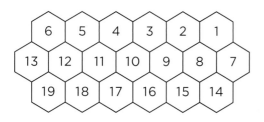

Here's a shapely trapezoid-ish wrap of 18 hex motifs, also approximately 66″ (168cm) long and 28″ (71cm) wide.

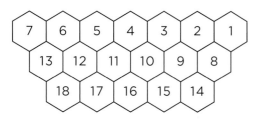

A little more yarn is needed to make 20 motifs for a diamond-ish throw, about 45″ (114cm) long by 38″ (96.5cm) wide.

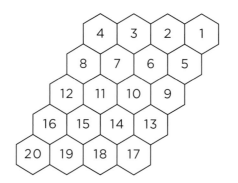

stella BLANKET WRAP

While you may certainly snuggle under a throw, or arrange it around your shoulders for a shawl, a flat piece doesn't become a functional garment until there are places for your arms. With Stella, made with twenty tiled hexagons, take a step toward garment construction. By leaving sections of motifs unconnected during assembly, you can make what is essentially a blanket with armholes, an upside-downable wrap, or a vest with a stay-put shape.

Size

Drapes to fit up to size XL

Finished length 54" (137cm); depth at center back 34" (86cm)

Materials

NaturallyCaron.com JOY!, 70% acrylic, 30% rayon from bamboo, 2½ oz (70g), 138 yd (125.5m) Medium

7 skeins in #0003 Sunset, or approximately 840 yd (764.5m) medium worsted weight yarn

U.S. Size I-9 (5.5mm) crochet hook or size needed to obtain gauge

Gauge

Constellation Major Hex Motif

RND 2: 3¼" (8cm) diameter

RND 6: one side, point to point = 5½" (14cm); height = 9" (23cm); widest point = 10" (25.5cm)

Please see Measuring Motifs (page 35).

Stitch Definitions

See instructions for individual Constellation major hex motifs (page 31).

For more motif assembly information, see Universal Assembly (page 33).

Instructions

MOTIFS 1–7: Make 7 Constellation major hex motifs, connecting them completely to one another as you go while crocheting the last round of each motif according to the assembly diagram.

Leave 5 ch-sps free (1 point space, 3 side spaces, and a 1 point space) at the outer edges of Motifs 8 and 9 for armholes.

MOTIF 8: *Do not connect at all to Motif 7; do not join to the lower point of Motif 2.* Work the first point sp unattached; skip the point join between Motifs 2 and 7; connect the next 3 side sps to Motif 2; and connect completely to Motif 3. Finish the rest of the motif.

MOTIF 9: *Do not join in the lower point of Motif 4.* Connect completely to Motifs 8 and 3, then connect the next 3 side sps to Motif 4. Finish the rest of the motif.

MOTIF 10: *Do not connect at all to Motif 9.* Connect completely to Motifs 4 and 5, then finish the rest of the motif.

MOTIFS 11 AND 12: Connect completely to the previous motifs.

MOTIF 13: Connect completely to Motifs 12 and 7; skip the free point of Motif 8, then connect the next 3 side sps to Motif 8. Finish the rest of the motif.

MOTIF 14: Connect completely to the previous motifs.

MOTIF 15: Connect completely to Motif 14, then connect the next 3 side sps to Motif 9. Skip the free point of Motif 9, and connect completely to Motif 10. Finish the rest of the motif.

MOTIFS 16–20: Connect completely to the previous motifs and to one another.

Weave in the ends, and block.

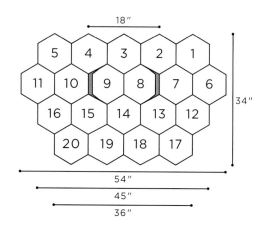

chaos WRAP

Another approach to creating body shaping in a flat piece is by angular construction. Chaos is still flat, but is V-shaped, with the long arms of the V folded over the shoulders to form "fronts." Feel free to play with colors. Chaos is made of nineteen hexagons using a very traditional color scheme, with multicolor centers set in a neutral background of outer rounds. But just because I am so matchy-matchy does not doom you to the same fate. Work any motif rounds in as many colors as you please—even mix in different yarns of similar weight. Let the Chaos ensue!

skill level

INTERMEDIATE ● ● ○

Size

One size fits most

Finished length, center back from back neck 17″ (43cm); length, one front from back neck 30″ (76cm); width, lower back 15″ (38cm); width, one front 15″ (38cm)

Materials

Kraemer Tatamy, 45% cotton, 55% acrylic, 3½ oz (100g), 250 yd (228m) (3) Light

2 skeins in Birch (MC)

Less than 1 oz (28g) used in each of five contrasting colors: Fireplace (brick red) (A); Ginger (orange) (B); Playtime (spring green) (C); Forest (dark forest green) (D);Teal (E)

U.S. Size H-8 (5mm) crochet hook or size needed to obtain gauge

Gauge

Copernicus Major Hex Motif

RND 3: 3¼″ (8cm) diameter

RND 4: 5½″ (14cm) diameter

RND 7: one side, point to point = 5″ (12.5cm); height = 8″ (20.5cm); widest point = 9½″ (24cm)

Please see Measuring Motifs (page 35).

Stitch Definitions

See instructions for individual Copernicus major hex motifs (page 23).

For more motif assembly information, see Universal Assembly (page 33).

Instructions

Make 19 two-color centers for 19 Copernicus major hex motifs (page 23) according to the color scheme shown in the assembly diagram, with the changes below for working with multiple yarns.

Two-Color Copernicus Hex Motif Centers

RNDS 1–3: With first color, work as written, then fasten off.

RND 4: Join the second color with sl st in same sc as you fastened off. Work Rnd 4 as written, then fasten off.

Assembly

Taking each center in color scheme order, complete the motifs and connect them to one another according to the assembly diagram.

MOTIF 1: With Motif 1 center and MC, join with sl st in the same top of the beginning ch as you fastened off; work Rnds 5–7 as written.

MOTIFS 2–19: With the next motif center in order and MC, join with sl st in the same top of the beginning ch as you fastened off; work Rnds 5–6 as written, then work Rnd 7, connecting them completely to one another.

Weave in the ends, and block.

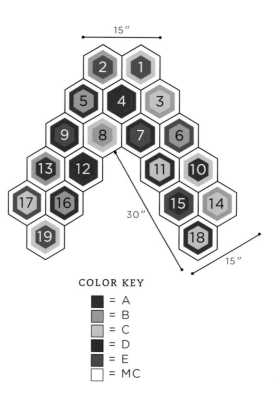

COLOR KEY

- = A
- = B
- = C
- = D
- = E
- = MC

miranda VEST

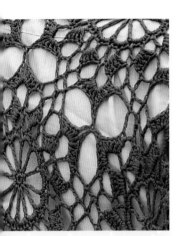

Notice how the Chaos Wrap (page 61) wants to meet at the sides. What if you connected or captured the edges of the lower motifs in fronts and back? Swapped out the yarn for a silky tape in one knockout shade? You'd get this slinky, stretchy, draped-front vest. To wear the vest closed in front, make a button stud (page 140) to slip through the front point spaces as desired.

skill level
INTERMEDIATE ● ● ○

Size
Stretch to fit bust up to 44″ (112cm)

Materials
South West Trading Company Oasis, 100% soy silk, 3½ oz (100g), 240 yd (219m) (3) Light

3 skeins in 065 Sapphire

U.S. Size H-8 (5mm) crochet hook or size needed to obtain gauge

Stitch markers

1″ (25mm) button or button stud (page 140) as desired

Gauge
Copernicus Minor Hex Motif

RND 3: 3¼″ (8cm) diameter

RND 6: one side, point to point = 4″ (10cm); height = 6½″ (16.5cm); widest point = 8″ (20.5cm)

Please see Measuring Motifs (page 35).

Stitch Definitions
See instructions for individual Copernicus minor hex motifs (page 23).

For more motif assembly information, see Universal Assembly (page 33).

Instructions

MOTIFS 1–9: Make 9 Copernicus minor hex motifs, connecting them completely to one another. Mark the point join between Motifs 1 and 3 and between Motifs 2 and 5.

MOTIF 11: Connect completely to Motifs 6 and 7.

MOTIF 10: Connect completely to Motif 6 and Motif 11, and work the next (2 side sps, point sp, and 2 side sps) unattached. Join the next point sp to the marked join of Motifs 1 and 3, and connect the next (2 side sps and point sp) to Motif 3. Finish the rest of the motif.

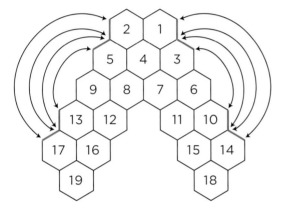

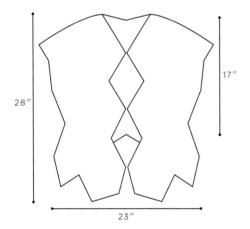

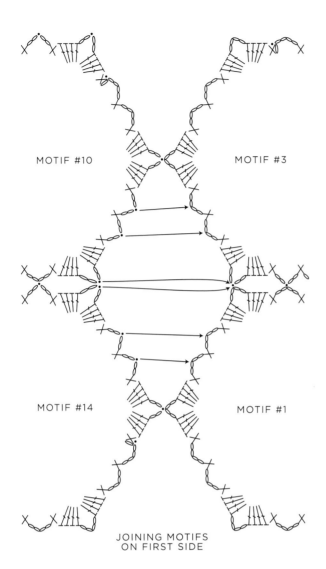

MOTIF #10   MOTIF #3

MOTIF #14   MOTIF #1

JOINING MOTIFS
ON FIRST SIDE

MOTIF 12: Connect completely to Motifs 8 and 9.

MOTIF 13: Connect completely to Motifs 12 and Motif 9, then work the next 2 side sps unattached. Join the next point sp to the remaining free point sp of Motif 5, and connect the next 2 side sps to Motif 5. Join the next point sp to the marked join of Motifs 2 and 5, and finish the rest of the motif.

MOTIF 15: Connect completely to Motifs 10 and 11.

MOTIF 14: Join the first point sp to the next free point sp of Motif 1, then connect the next 2 side sps to Motif 1 (*moving toward the marker*). Join the next point to marked join of Motifs 1 and 3 (*yes, there are 4 points joined at this place*), then connect the next 2 side sps to Motif 10. Connect completely to Motif 15, and finish the rest of the motif.

MOTIF 16: Connect completely to Motifs 12 and 13.

MOTIF 17: Connect completely to Motif 16, then join the next 2 side sps to Motif 13. Join the next point sp to the marked join of Motifs 2 and 5 (*yes, there are 4 points joined at this place*). Connect the next (2 side sps and point sp) to the next (2 side sps and free point) of Motif 2. Finish the rest of the motif.

MOTIFS 18–19: Connect completely to previous motifs.

Weave in the ends, and block.

Make a button stud (page 140) to close the front as desired.

POLYGONZO:
pentagons

Of all the polygons in the family, pentagons are my favorite children, the stubborn oddballs. Pents do not play well with others; they will not tile no matter what you do with them. Connected to each other or to any of their siblings, pents encourage the fabric to warp, curl, curve, and otherwise wander off the two dimensions of a plane. Rather than fight it, we can use the plane-busting power of pents for three-dimensional garment shaping.

galaxy SKIRT

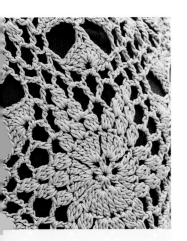

The mix of textured five- and six-pointed stars gives this pull-on skirt its shapely hip. The Galaxy Skirt waistband uses a brilliant technique for running a fine strand of elastic along with the yarn for a snug, fitted waist. Slim fitting and knee length, this skirt may be easily lengthened to below the knee by adding another course of motifs to the bottom.

skill level
INTERMEDIATE ● ● ○

Size
XS/S (M/L, XL), sample shown size XS/S
Finished full hip 39 (45½, 52)″ (99 [115.5, 132] cm); waist (unstretched) 24 (27, 31)″ (61 [68.5, 79]cm), adjustable; length 20″ (51cm)

Materials
Tahki Cotton Classic Lite, 100% mercerized cotton, 1¾ oz (50g), 146 yd (135m) (**2**) Fine
5 (6, 7) hanks in 4809 Teal
Rainbow Elastic (Bryson Distributing), 1 mm Fine; 50 yd (45m) per card
1 (2, 2) cards in #44 Deep Peacock
U.S. Size G-6 (4mm) crochet hook or size needed to obtain gauge

Gauge
18 fsc or fdc = 4″ (10cm)

Constellation Major Pent Motif
RND 1: 2″ (5cm)
RND 2: 3″ (7.5cm) diameter at the widest point
RND 5: one side, point to point = 4¼″ (11cm); height = 6″ (15cm); widest point = 6½″ (16.5cm)

Constellation Major Hex Motif
RND 2: 2½″ (6.5cm)
RND 6: one side, point to point = 4¼″ (11cm); height = 6½″ (16.5cm); widest point = 8″ (20.5cm)

Please see Measuring Motifs (page 35).

In the slip stitch ribbing of waistband, 10 sl st = 2″ (5cm) as crocheted; this will compress to 1¼″ (3cm) waistband depth

18 rows sl st through the bottom loop only = 3½″ (9cm), with plenty of bounce-back stretch

Stitch Definitions
FSC (FOUNDATION SINGLE CROCHET), FDC (FOUNDATION DOUBLE CROCHET: See Chainless Foundations (page 140).

SL ST THROUGH BACK LOOP ONLY: See Slip Stitch Ribbing (page 72).

See instructions for individual Constellation motifs (page 29).

For more motif assembly information, see Universal Assembly (page 33).

Pattern Notes
Cotton yarn shrinks slightly after wetting and drying as blocked, but will relax again when worn to meet stated dimensions.

Slip Stitch Ribbing

Slip stitch ribbing is a wonderful thing. Worked through the back loop only (the strand on the far side of the previous row), it gives the appearance of knitted K1P1 ribbing. Ribbing using cotton (nonstretch) yarn, whether knit or crocheted, has stretch, but will generally stretch out and stay stretched out, because it has no elasticity. Manufacturers often run a strand of elastic along with the yarn in sweater bands and sock cuffs. You can do that in crochet, too, for a smooth, flexible, flat elastic waistband: no casing, no sewing, no rolling of elastic, no extra bulk.

The ribbing is worked sideways onto the upper edge of the waist. Traditional sideways methods travel down the wrong side (private side) of the band toward the skirt body, where the row is attached with slip stitching to the wrong side of the piece, then the work is turned to the right side for the trip back up the ribbing. In slip stitch ribbing this makes an unnecessarily bumpy connection to the skirt waist.

Try this method instead. Work on the right side of the ribbing toward the skirt waist, then turn. Bring the feeder yarn to the back of the row to prepare for the next step. Moving backward (which will feel really weird at first), slip stitch in the indicated stitches of the skirt waist on the wrong side; then move forward and con-

tinue the row back up the ribbing on the wrong side. The messy turning bump magically disappears.

Slip stitches tend to lie flat against the row. After turning, the tops of the previous row are tilted to the back of the work. To find the back loop of each stitch, you may have to dig way into the back of the row. The first and last slip stitches in a row can be squished, hidden, and easily missed, so check your count occasionally.

Keep slip stitches relaxed and even. The temptation is to work each row tighter and tighter. Resist. It should never be a struggle to insert the hook in the next loop. Make sure you work in both the yarn strand and the elastic strand each time.

For the most extreme shaped waist style, each row of ribbing takes up one stitch of waist edge. This might seem to result in too few rows around, but once the ribbing settles, stretches, and settles again, you should see the correct waistband proportions. For a more relaxed elastic waist, you may insert extra ribbing rows as suggested in the instructions. For absolute control of the waistband, forgo the elastic style and add the drawstring waistband option as shown in the Kerry Skirt (page 122).

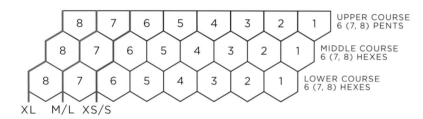

UPPER COURSE
6 (7, 8) PENTS

MIDDLE COURSE
6 (7, 8) HEXES

LOWER COURSE
6 (7, 8) HEXES

XL   M/L   XS/S

Working with Carry-along Elastic

Fine Rainbow Elastic (1mm) is as fine as crochet thread and does not add noticeable bulk to the crochet when carried with the main yarn. Rainbow Elastic is generously packaged with 50 yards (45 meters) on a card for around three dollars per card. It comes in forty-eight colors. Rainbow, right? Chances are you can find a close match to your yarn for near invisibility. I got majorly lucky with this skirt sample, but the manufacturer suggests that if you can't get a good match, choose a shade of elastic a click darker than the yarn.

One tricky aspect is that the elastic strand can get hung up as you draw it off the card. To encourage the elastic to feed at the same tension as the yarn, I suggest rewinding the elastic into a loose ball or butterfly hank and keeping it in a plastic bag. You can't avoid stretching the elastic as you crochet, nor can you keep the elastic and yarn feeds from getting twisted together. Don't worry about either. When you're done, treat the loose ends of elastic as you would yarn ends, threading them on a tapestry needle and weaving them into the crochet stitches.

Instructions

Assemble 18 (24, 28) motifs, connecting each motif as you go while crocheting the last round, assembled in three courses.

UPPER COURSE: Make 6 (7, 8) Constellation major pent motifs, completely connected to one another in a ring, with one flat side of each motif at the waist, the pointed end at the hip.

MIDDLE COURSE: Make 6 (7, 8) Constellation major hex motifs, completely connected to the upper course of pents and to one another.

LOWER COURSE: Make 6 (7, 8) Constellation major hex motifs completely connected to the middle course of hexes and to one another.

Weave in the ends.

FIT TIP: *For a longer skirt, make and connect another course of hex motifs for approximately 5" (12.5cm) additional length at this gauge.*

Elastic Waistband
Waist Foundation

Fsc 120 (140, 160) to measure approximately 27 (31, 35½)" (68.5 [79, 90]cm). *(To measure, stretch the foundation, let it snap back if it wants to, and measure end to end.)* Bring the ends of the foundation together, being care-ful not to twist the stitches, then sl st in first sc to form a ring. Begin to work across sc edge of the foundation.

With the right side of the skirt body facing, hold the foundation ring to the left (nonhook side) and the skirt edge to the hook side. Bouncing back and forth, as you would to connect motif sides, connect the foundation to the ch-4 sps of 6 (7, 8) sides of the pent motifs at the upper edge, using 20 foundation stitches per motif side. Begin with the first connection in the partial ch-sp just past any join between motifs.

TIP: *Just before closing the following Connecting Rnd, bring the feeder yarn to the wrong side of the work, so it is in the proper place to continue the waistband.*

WAIST CONNECTING RND (RS): Ch 1, sc in the first sc of the foundation; *ch 2, sl st in the partial ch-sp past the motif join; [ch 2, skip next 3 sc of the foundation, sc in the next sc; ch 2, sl st in the next ch-4 sp of the motif] 3 times; ch 2, skip the next 3 sc of the foundation, sc in the next sc; ch 2, sl st in the next partial ch-sp before the motif join; ch 2, skip the next 3 sc of the foundation; sc in the next sc*; repeat from * to * 5 (6, 7) times; on the final repeat, omit the last sc; instead, sl st in the beginning sc—30 (35, 40) ch-sp joins.

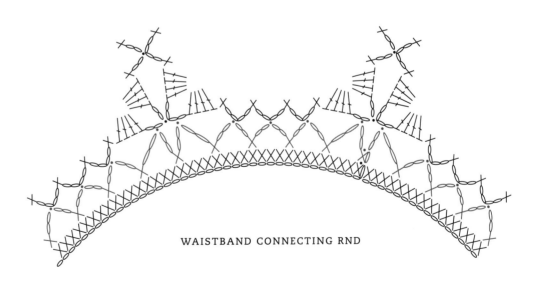

WAISTBAND CONNECTING RND

Rotate your work so the chain edge of the foundation is on top (the feeder yarn is now to the wrong side, the inside of the skirt). Sl st in the stem of the same beginning sc (the one just joined in); sl st in the loops of the foundation sc just above; sl st in the chain of the foundation.

Elastic Ribbing

With the right side still facing, and holding the yarn together with a strand of fine elastic, work sl st ribbing sideways around the ch edge of the foundation, making one row of ribbing for each ch.

ROW 1 (RS): Ch 11 *(this equals 10 sts plus 1 edge st)*, do not turn; rotate the piece to work across the right-side face of the chains.

ROW 2 (RS): Skip the first ch from the hook; sl st through the back loop only *(for this row only the back loop is the one on top)* in each of the next 10 chs; turn—10 sl st.

ROW 3 (WS): With the feeder yarn to the back of work as usual, moving backward, and working in the top loops of the foundation ch edge, sl st in each of the next 2 chains, then moving forward, skip 2 sl sts just made, and sl st through the back loop only *(the bottom loop all the way in back)* in each of the 10 sl sts; turn.

ROW 4 (RS): Ch 1, skip ch 1; sl st through the back loop only in each of the next 10 sl st; turn.

Repeat Rows 3–4 around the chain edge of the foundation. At the end of a Row 4 with one ch left, sl st backward in the last ch of the edge.

TIP: *For a more relaxed elastic waistband, add ribbing rows by adjusting Row 3. Instead of sl st in 2 chains of foundation, sl st in only one ch; then, moving forward, skip that sl st and sl st through the back loop only as usual. Do this at evenly spaced intervals around. For every 5 rows added in this way you will increase the waistband by about 1" (2.5cm).*

Cut the yarn and the elastic, leaving a long tail of yarn for seaming; pull the tail through the last slip stitch. Leave the elastic tail for weaving in later; thread the yarn tail on the tapestry needle.

I think the seaming looks better when done on the right side of the band, but you may do it any way you please. Holding the 10 slip stitches of the last row side by side with the spare loops of the 10 chains of Row 1 and matching loops, mattress stitch the edges together, bouncing from the back loop of the slip stitch edge to the spare loop, being careful to keep the stitches relaxed. Take a stitch into the end of the seam to secure, then fasten off. Weave in the ends.

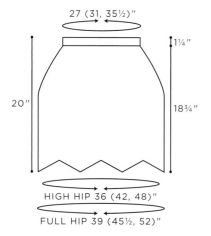

27 (31, 35½)"

1¼"

20"

18¾"

HIGH HIP 36 (42, 48)"

FULL HIP 39 (45½, 52)"

titan TOP

Pentagons will lend 3-D shaping to the neck and shoulders of a top. This lacy topper of twelve exploded gauge motifs features a wide boatneck and cap shoulders. The fit of the top is oversize, very relaxed, with the body curving gracefully to a soft, wide, ribbed band that falls to the hip and holds in some of the fullness. For a smaller or larger waist, make adjustments in the ribbing as suggested in the instructions.

Size

S/M (L/XL), sample shown is size S/M

Finished bust at dropped underarm 48 (52)" (122 [132]cm); waist above ribbing 32 (40)" (81 [102]cm); ribbed band 27 (34)" (68.5 [86]cm); length 21 (23)" (53.5 [58.5]cm)

Materials

Berroco Weekend, 75% acrylic, 25% Peruvian cotton, 3½ oz (100g), 205 yd (187m) (4) Medium

3 (4) hanks 5956 Swimming Hole (peacock)

U.S. Size J-10 (6mm) crochet hook or size needed to obtain gauge

Gauge

12 fdc or sc = 4" (10cm)

For Size S/M

Constellation Minor Pent Motif
RND 1: 2¾" (7cm)

RND 4: one side, point to point = 5" (12.5cm); height = 8" (20.5cm); widest point = 8½" (21.5cm)

Constellation Minor Hex Motif
RND 2: 3½" (9cm)

RND 5: one side, point to point = 5" (12.5cm); height = 8" (20.5cm); widest point = 9" (23cm)

For Size L/XL

Constellation Major Pent Motif
RND 1: 2¾" (7cm)

RND 5: one side, point to point = 6" (15cm); height = 9" (23cm); widest point = 10" (25.5cm)

Constellation Major Hex Motif
RND 2: 3½" (9cm)

RND 6: one side, point to point = 6" (15cm); height = 8½" (21.5cm); widest point = 11" (28cm)

Please see Measuring Motifs (page 35).

In sl st ribbing as crocheted, 15 sl st = 4" (10cm); 16 rows = 4" (10cm); the ribbing will compress in stitch gauge to 20 sts of band = 4" (10cm); the row gauge will stretch to 14 rows = 4" (10cm) to give finished measurements.

Stitch Definitions

FDC (FOUNDATION DOUBLE CROCHET): See Chainless Foundations (page 140).

See instructions for individual Constellation motifs (page 29).

For more motif assembly information, see Universal Assembly (page 33).

For more about slip stitch ribbing, see Galaxy Skirt (page 71).

Instructions

Size S/M uses Constellation minor motifs.

Size L/XL uses Constellation major motifs.

Assemble 12 motifs, connecting each motif as you go while crocheting the last round, according to the assembly diagram in the same way for both sizes. Numbers are written for size S/M, with changes for L/XL in parentheses.

Upper Course (neckline and shoulders)

MOTIFS 1–6: Make four pent and two hex motifs. Connect them completely to one another to form a ring, with one flat side of each motif at the neckline, and one hex at each shoulder.

Lower Course

MOTIFS 7–9: Make two hex and one center pent motifs. Connect them completely to the upper course and to one another to form one half of the body.

Rotate the work to assemble the other half of the body, folding at the shoulder line and curving the sides of the body to meet.

MOTIF 10 (HEX): Connect completely to Motif 9 at the side of the body. Work the next 2 (3) side ch-sps unattached for the armhole opening. Join the next point sp to the next free point sp of Motif 3, then connect the next side and point sp completely to the next side of Motif 3. Connect the next side completely to the next side of Motif 4; then finish the rest of the motif.

MOTIF 11 (PENT): Connect completely at the center of the body to Motif 10, Motif 4, and Motif 5. Finish the rest of the motif.

MOTIF 12 (HEX): Connect completely to Motif 11, Motif 5, and Motif 6. Work the next 2 (3) side ch-sps unattached for the armhole opening, then join the next point sp to the next free point sp of Motif 7. Connect the next side and point completely to Motif 7 at the side of the body; then finish the rest of the motif.

Weave in the ends.

Finishing
Neckline

The loose neckline edge is controlled with a narrow band, a ring of foundation stitches connected to the neck edge of the motifs with ch-sps as you would connect motifs to one another.

Fdc 72 (90) to measure approximately 24 (30)" (61 [76]cm). *(To measure, stretch the foundation, let it snap back if it wants to, and measure end to end.)* Bring the ends of the foundation together, being careful not to twist the stitches, and sl st in the beginning dc (in the 4th chain of the beginning ch) to form a ring. Begin work across the dc edge of the foundation.

With the right side of the motifs facing, hold the foundation ring to the nonhook side and the neck edge to the hook side. Bouncing back and forth, as you would to connect motif sides, connect the foundation to the ch-4 sps of 6 sides of the motifs at the neck edge, using 12 (15) foundation stitches per motif side. Begin with the first connection in the partial ch-sp at one shoulder, just past the join between Motifs 1 and 6.

NECK CONNECTING RND (RS): Ch 1, sc in the first dc of the foundation; *ch 2, sl st in the partial ch-sp past the motif join; [ch 2, skip

ASSEMBLY DIAGRAM

the next 2 dc of the foundation, sc in the next dc; ch 2, sl st in the next ch-4 sp of the motif] 2 (3) times; ch 2, skip the next 2 dc of the foundation, sc in the next dc; ch 2, sl st in the next partial ch-sp before the motif join; ch 2, skip the next 2 dc of the foundation, sc in the next dc*; repeat from * to * 5 times; on the final repeat, omit the last sc; instead, sl st in the beginning sc. Fasten off—24 (30) ch-sp joins.

The fdc has height. It is already connected across the dc edge; now, while weaving in the beginning tail, connect the chain edge. Thread the beginning tail onto a tapestry needle, reach across the gap in the foundation, and loop it around the last chain of the foundation. Weave in the ends.

Armholes

The armhole openings are bound proportionally more generously than the neckline for a roomy fit around the upper arm.

Fdc 48 (60), to measure approximately 16 (20)" (40.5 [51]cm). *(To measure, stretch the foundation, let it snap back if it wants to, and measure end to end.)* Bring the ends of the foundation together, being careful not to twist the stitches. Sl st in the beginning dc (in the 4th chain of the beginning ch) to form a ring. Connect the foundation to one armhole opening using 16 (20) foundation stitches per motif side. Begin with the first connection in the partial ch-sp at one underarm, just past the motif join.

ARMHOLE CONNECTING RND (RS): Ch 1, sc in the first dc of the foundation; *ch 2, sl st in the partial ch-sp past the motif join; [ch 2, skip the next 3 dc of the foundation, sc in the next dc; ch 2, sl st in the next ch-4 sp of motif] 2 (3) times; ch 2, skip the next 3 dc of the foundation, sc in the next dc; ch 2, sl st in the next partial ch-sp before the motif join; ch 2, skip the next 3 dc of the foundation, sc in the next stitch*; repeat from * to * 2 times; on the final repeat, omit the last sc; instead, sl st in the beginning sc. Fasten off—12 (15) ch-sp joins.

Make and connect the band around the other armhole opening in same way. Finish and weave the foundation ends in same way as for the neck band.

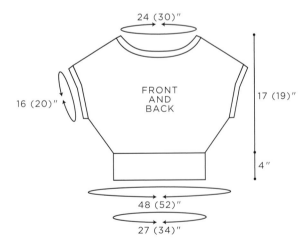

24 (30)"

16 (20)"

FRONT AND BACK

17 (19)"

4"

48 (52)"

27 (34)"

Waistband

Begin to control the waist with the following finishing rounds across the sides of the 6 motifs at the lower edge.

With the right side facing, join yarn with a sl st in the partial ch-sp just past the join between two hex motifs at the side of the body.

RND 1 (RS): Ch 1, sc in the same sp;* [ch 4, sc in the next ch-4 sp] 2 (3) times; ch 4, sc in the next partial ch-sp before the motif join; ch 4, sc in the next partial ch-sp after the motif join*; repeat from * to * 5 times; on the final repeat, omit the last sc; instead, sl st in the beginning sc—24 (30) ch-4 sps.

RND 2 (RS): Ch 1; 4 sc in each ch-4 sp around; sl st in the beginning sc—96 (120) sc.

FIT TIP: *For a looser or tighter waistband, adjust the number of sc stitches in Rnd 2 of the waist finishing. Instead of 4 sc stitches in every ch-4 sp, make 5 sc stitches in some ch-4 sps for more waistband ribbing rows, or 3 sc in some ch-4 sps for fewer ribbing rows. Work the increases or decreases this way as many times as desired, evenly spaced around. 3 sc will translate to approximately 1" (2.5cm) change in waistband ribbing; end with an even number of sc stitches.*

With the right side still facing, work slip stitch ribbing sideways around the sc edge, making one row of ribbing for each sc.

ROW 1 (RS): Ch 21 (*this equals 20 sts plus 1 edge st*); do not turn; rotate the piece to work across the right-side face of the chain.

ROW 2 (RS): Skip the first chain from the hook, sl st through the back loop only (*for this row only the back loop is the one on top*) in each of the 20 chains and turn—20 sl sts.

ROW 3 (WS): Moving backward, sl st in each of the next 2 sc stitches of the waist edge; then, moving forward, skip the 2 sl sts just made; sl st through the back loop only (*the bottom loop all the way in back*) in each of the 20 sl sts; turn.

ROW 4 (RS): Ch 1, skip ch 1 stitch, and sl st through the back loop only in each of the 20 sl sts; turn.

Repeat Rows 3–4 around the sc edge of the waist. At the end of a Row 4, sl st backward in the last sc stitch of the edge.

Cut the yarn, leaving a long tail for seaming. Pull the tail through the last slip stitch, and thread the yarn tail on a tapestry needle. Seam the 20 stitches of the band in the same way as the Galaxy Skirt waistband, page 74.

Weave in the ends, and block.

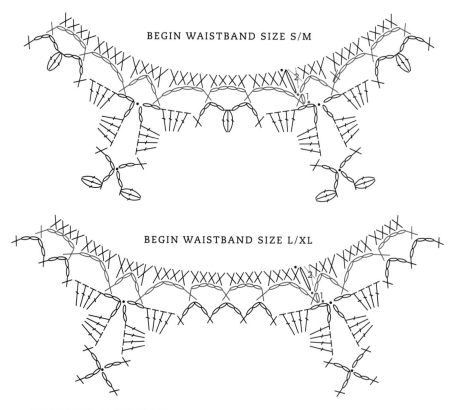

BEGIN WAISTBAND SIZE S/M

BEGIN WAISTBAND SIZE L/XL

zodiac TUNIC

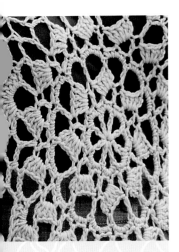

Even the most stubborn pentagons can be made to bend to the will of mighty octagons, as used to stunning effect with Zodiac. This relaxed dolman-shaped tunic places huge Copernicus octs at the center of the body, ringed with Copernicus pents. Octs also form the sleeves.

skill level
EXPERIENCED ● ● ●

Size

Average (Plus); oversize fit for S/M/L (XL/2XL) for body bust up to 42 (50)" (106.5 [127]cm); sample shown is size Average

Finished body at dropped dolman underarm 52 (56)" (132 [142]cm); length from neckline to the center front 22 (24)" (56 [61]cm); total length 27(29)" (68.5 [74]cm)

Materials

Filatura Di Crosa Zara, 100% superwash merino wool, 1¾ oz (50g), 137 yd (125m) **3** Light

6 (8) balls in #1451 Oatmeal

U.S. Size H-8 (5mm) crochet hook or size needed to obtain gauge

Stitch markers

Gauge

14 fdc = 4" (10cm) as crocheted; will stretch slightly with blocking and wearing to 13 fdc = 4" (10cm)

For Size Average

Copernicus Minor Pent Motif

RND 3: 3½" (9cm)

RND 6: one side, point to point = 5" (12.5cm); height = 8" (20.5cm); widest point = 8½" (21.5cm)

Copernicus Minor Oct Motif

RND 2: 2¾" (7cm)

RND 5: 6½" (16.5cm)

RND 8: one side, point to point = 5" (12.5cm); height = 10" (25.5cm); widest point = 12" (30.5cm)

For Size Plus

Copernicus Major Pent Motif

RND 3: 3½" (9cm)

RND 7: one side, point to point = 5½" (14cm); height = 8½" (21.5cm); widest point = 9" (23cm)

Copernicus Major Oct Motif

RND 2: 2¾" (7cm)

RND 5: 6½" (16.5cm)

RND 8: one side, point to point = 5½" (14cm); height = 11" (28cm); widest point = 13" (33cm)

Please see Measuring Motifs (page 35).

Stitch Definitions

FDC (FOUNDATION DOUBLE CROCHET): See Chainless Foundations (page 140).

See instructions for individual Copernicus motifs (page 22).

For more motif assembly information, see Universal Assembly (page 33).

Pattern Note

The front and back body of Zodiac are visually the same, but will be assembled differently, so by convention, one half is designated the front and the other becomes the back. Each body piece has one oct motif in the center of and 7 pents connected at 7 of the oct sides around, leaving one oct side open at the neck.

Instructions

Size Average uses Copernicus minor octs and Copernicus minor pents.

Size Plus uses Copernicus major octs and Copernicus major pents.

Make and assemble 18 Copernicus minor (major) motifs according to assembly diagram.

Front

MOTIF 1 (BODY OCT): Make one oct complete.

MOTIFS 2–8: Make 7 pents, connecting them to one another and to Motif 1 as you go. The one oct side remaining open is the center front neck. Pent Motifs 2 and 8 are the shoulders.

Back

MOTIF 9 (OCT): Make one oct complete.

Mark the outer point joins between Motifs 3 and 4 and between Motifs 6 and 7. With the right sides facing and with the front to the hook hand side and Motif 9 to the nonhook side, make and connect 7 pents to Motif 9, to one another, and to their corresponding motifs of the front at the shoulders and body sides.

MOTIF 10 (PENT): Connect completely to the upper edge of Motif 8 (at shoulder line), then work the next 2 (3) side sps unattached. Connect completely to Motif 9 and finish the rest of the motif.

MOTIF 11 (PENT): Connect completely to Motif 10 and to the next side of Motif 9, then work the next 2 (3) side sps unattached. Folding at

the shoulder line to make this next bit easier, join the next point sp to the marked join between Motifs 6 and 7, then connect the next 2 (3) side sps to Motif 7 (up the side of the body). Join the next point sp to the free point sp of Motif 7 (at the underarm), then finish the rest of the motif.

MOTIF 12 (PENT): Join the first point sp to the free point sp of Motif 6 (the bottom of the body), then connect the next 2 (3) side sps to Motif 6 (up the side of the body). Join the next point sp to the marked join between Motifs 6 and 7, then connect the next 2 (3) side sps to Motif 11. Connect completely to the next side of Motif 9, then finish the rest of the motif.

MOTIF 13 (PENT): Connect completely to Motif 12 and to the next side of Motif 9, then finish the rest of the motif.

MOTIF 14 (PENT): Connect completely to Motif 13 and to the next side of Motif 9. Work the next 2 (3) side sps unattached, then join the next point sp to the marked join between Motifs 3 and 4. Connect the next 2 (3) side sps to Motif 4 (down the side of the body), then join the next point sp to the free point sp of Motif 4 (the bottom of the body), and finish the rest of the motif.

MOTIF 15 (PENT): Join the first point sp to the free point sp of Motif 3 (at the underarm), then connect the next 2 (3) side sps to Motif 3 (down the side of the body). Join the next point sp to the marked join between Motifs 3 and 4, then connect the next 2 (3) side sps to Motif 14. Connect completely to the next side of Motif 9, and finish the rest of the motif.

ASSEMBLY DIAGRAM

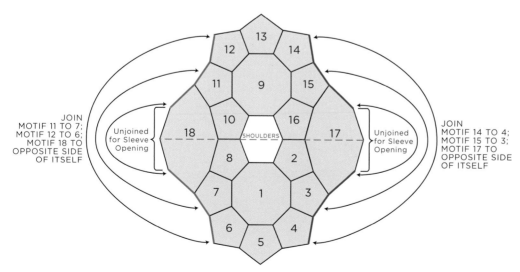

JOIN
MOTIF 11 TO 7;
MOTIF 12 TO 6;
MOTIF 18 TO
OPPOSITE SIDE
OF ITSELF

Unjoined for Sleeve Opening

SHOULDERS

Unjoined for Sleeve Opening

JOIN
MOTIF 14 TO 4;
MOTIF 15 TO 3;
MOTIF 17 TO
OPPOSITE SIDE
OF ITSELF

pletely to the next sides of Motifs 15, 16 and 2. Connect the next 2 (3) side sps to Motif 3, then join the next point sp to the same underarm join between Motifs 15 and 3. Folding the sleeve in half, connect the motif to itself by connecting the next 2 (3) side sps to the first unattached side sps of the motif. Join the next point sp to the first point sp made. Finish the rest of the motif.

MOTIF 18 (OCT): Work the first point sp and the next 2 (3) side sps unattached. Join the next point sp to the join at the underarm between Motifs 7 and 11, then connect completely to the next sides of Motifs 7, 8, and 10. Connect the next 2 (3) side sps to Motif 11, then join the next point sp to the same underarm join between Motifs 11 and 7. Folding the sleeve in half, connect the motif to itself by connecting the next 2 (3) side sps to the first unattached side sps of the motif. Join the next point sp to the first point sp made. Finish the rest of the motif.

Weave in the ends.

Neck Finishing

The Zodiac neck opening needs special binding in order to stay on the shoulders. This finishing will fill in the angles, hold in some of the fullness, and shape the U at the front and the back neck.

There is an unconnected oct motif side at the center of the front and center of the back. For size Average, mark the sc in the middle of the minor oct side; for size Plus, mark the ch-4 sp in the middle of the major oct side.

Fdc 80 (92); bring the ends of the foundation together, being careful not to twist the stitches. Sl st in the beginning dc (in the 4th ch of the beginning ch 4) to form a ring, then begin to work across the dc edge.

Size Average Only

The first round begins at what corresponds to the center of the back neck, and results in a ch-4 sp at the center point of the front neck and back neck.

RND 1 (RS): Ch 1, sc in the first dc; ch 4, skip the next 3 dc, sc in the next dc; *ch 4, skip the next dc, sc in the next dc; [ch 4, skip the next 3 dc, sc in the next dc] 3 times*; repeat from * to *; ch 4, skip the next dc, dc in the next dc; ch 4, skip the next 3 dc; and sc in the next dc; ch 4, skip the next dc (the other point of the V-neck), sc in the next dc, ch 4,

MOTIF 16 (PENT): Connect completely to Motif 15 and to next side of Motif 9, then work the next 2 (3) side sps unattached. Connect completely to the upper edge of Motif 2 (at the shoulder line), and finish the rest of the motif.

Sleeves

With the right side facing, fit one oct into each armhole opening, connecting four sides to the four motif sides of the armhole, and connecting two sides to each other as the underside of the sleeve, leaving two sides open at the bottom of the sleeve.

MOTIF 17 (OCT): Work the first point sp and the next 2 (3) side sps unattached. Join the next point sp to the join at the underarm between Motifs 15 and 3, then connect com-

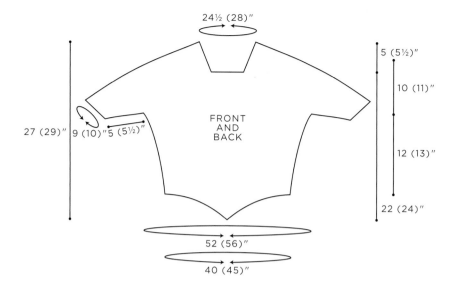

24½ (28)"

5 (5½)"

10 (11)"

27 (29)" 9 (10)" 5 (5½)"

FRONT
AND
BACK

12 (13)"

22 (24)"

52 (56)"

40 (45)"

skip the next 3 dc, sc in the next dc; repeat from * to * 2 times; ch 4, skip the next dc, sc in the next dc; ch 4, skip the next 3 dc, sc in the next dc; skip the last dc, ch 1, dc in the beginning sc *(this equals ch 4)*—24 ch-4 sps.

With the right side of pieces facing, connect the ch-4 sps of the foundation to the motif sides of neck opening beginning at the marker at the center of one neck oct side.

RND 2 (RS): Ch 1, sc in the beginning sp, ch 2, sl st in the next ch-4 sp past marked sc at the center of the neck motif side, ch 2, sc in the next ch-4 sp of foundation, *(no ch 4 here)* (4 dc, ch 2, sl st in the next join between motifs, ch 2, 4 dc) in the next ch-4 sp of the foundation, *(no ch-4 here)* sc in the next ch-4 sp of foundation**, [ch 2, sl st in the next ch-4 sp of motif, ch 2, sc in the next ch-4 sp of the foundation] twice*; repeat from * to * four more times, repeat from * to ** once, end with ch 2, sl st in the last ch-4 sp of motif, ch 2, sl st in beginning sc of the foundation, fasten off.

Size Plus Only

The first round begins at what corresponds to just before the center of the back neck, and results in a sc at the center point of the front neck and the back neck.

RND 1 (RS): Ch 1, sc in the first dc; ch 4, skip the next dc, sc in the next dc; ch 4, skip the next 3 dc, sc in the next dc; *ch 4, skip the next dc, sc in the next dc; ch 4, skip the next 3 dc, sc in the next dc; [ch 4, skip the next 2 dc, sc in the next dc] 2 times; ch 4, skip next 3 dc, sc in the next dc*; repeat from * to

*; ch 4, skip the next dc, sc in the next dc; ch 4, skip the next 3 dc, sc in the next dc; [ch 4, skip next dc, sc in the next dc] 2 times, ch 4, skip the next 3 dc, sc in the next dc; repeat from * to * 2 times; ch 4, skip the next dc, sc in the next dc; ch 4, skip the next 3 dc, sc in the next dc, skip the last dc; ch 1, dc in the beginning sc *(this equals ch 4)*—30 ch-4 sps.

With the right sides of the pieces facing, connect the ch-4 sps of the foundation to the motif sides of the neck opening, beginning at the marker at the center of one neck oct side.

RND 2 (RS): Ch 1, sc in the beginning sp, ch 2; Sl st in the marked ch-4 sp at the center of the neck motif side; ch 2, sc in the next ch-4 sp of the foundation; ch 2, sl st in the next ch-4 sp of the motif; ch 2, sc in the next ch-4 sp of the foundation *(no ch 4 here)* [4 dc, ch 2, sl st in the next join between the motifs; ch 2, 4 dc] in the next ch-4 sp of the foundation; *(no ch-4 here)* sc in the next ch-4 sp of the foundation**; [ch 2, sl st in the next ch-4 sp of the motif; ch 2, sc in the next ch-4 sp of the foundation] 2 (3) times*; repeat from * to * four times, then repeat from * to **; ch 2, sl st in the last ch-4 sp of the motif; ch 2, sl st in the beginning sc of the foundation. Fasten off.

Weave in the ends, and block.

callisto TOP

Callisto is a tiny satellite of Zodiac, crocheted in a finer gauge for a waist-cropped sleeveless top or rib-tickler vest. The scheme of three colors gives the Carina motifs a less angular appearance, so Callisto has a distinctly retro-floral appeal.

skill level
EXPERIENCED ● ● ●

Size

XS/S (M/L, XL/2X); sample shown is size XS/S

Finished bust 36 (42, 50)″ (91 [106.5, 127]cm); waist 30 (36, 45)″ (76 [91, 114]cm); length 17 (20, 20)″ (43 [51, 51]cm)

Materials

Elsebeth Lavold Hempathy, 34% hemp, 41% cotton, 25% modal, 1¾ oz (50g), 154 yd (141m) **1** Super Fine

2 (3, 3) balls in #37 Dark Linen (MC); 1 ball in #4 White Beach (A); 1 (2, 2) balls in #42 Snow Shadow (B)

U.S. Size G-6 (4mm) crochet hook or size needed to obtain gauge

Stitch markers

Gauge

For Size XS/S

Carina Minor Pent Motif

RND 1: 1⅜″ (3.5cm)

RND 2: 2½″ (6.5cm)

RND 5: one side, point to point = 3¼″ (8cm); height = 5″ (12.5cm); widest point = 5½″ (14cm)

Carina Minor Oct Motif

RND 2: 2¾″ (7cm)

RND 7: one side, point to point = 3¼″ (8cm); height = 7½″ (19cm); widest point = 8½″ (21.5cm)

For Sizes M/L and XL/2X

Carina Major Pent Motif

RND 1: 1⅜″ (3.5cm)

RND 2: 2½″ (6.5cm)

RND 6: one side, point to point = 4″ (10cm); height = 6″ (15cm); widest point = 6½″ (16.5cm)

Carina Major Oct Motif

RND 2: 2¾″ (7cm)

RND 8: one side, point to point = 4″ (10cm); height = 8½″ (21.5cm); widest point = 9½″ (24cm)

Carina Major Square Motif

RND 1: 1½″ (3.8cm)

RND 2: 2¼″ (5.5cm) wide

RND 5: one side, point to point = 4″ (10cm)

Please see Measuring Motifs (page 35).

Stitch Definitions

AIR DC (ALSO KNOWN AS A STANDING DC): Begin new yarn with a slip knot on the hook, YO, insert the hook in the st or sp as indicated, YO and draw up a loop, [YO and draw through 2 loops on hook] 2 times.

AIR SC (ALSO KNOWN AS A STANDING SC): Begin new yarn with a slip knot on the hook, insert the hook in the st or sp as indicated, YO and draw up a loop, YO and draw through the 2 loops on the hook.

See instructions for individual Carina motifs (page 25).

For more motif assembly information, see Universal Assembly (page 33) and the assembly instructions for Zodiac Tunic (page 81).

Instructions
Motif Centers

Make the following adjustments in the Carina motif general instructions to work with color changes. Begin by making all of the motif centers using colors A and B; the outer rounds will be completed in MC during assembly.

All Sizes Carina Pent Centers (Make 14)

With A, ch 6; sl st in the beginning chain to form a ring.

RND 1: Continuing with A, ch 3 *(this equals dc)*, 2 dc in the ring; [ch 2, 3 dc in the ring] 4 times; ch 2, sl st in the 3rd ch of the beginning ch. Fasten off A—5 ch-2 sps.

RND 2: With B, (air dc, 2 dc) in any ch-2 sp of Rnd 1; ch 2, [(3 dc, ch 2, 3 dc) in the next ch-2 sp; ch 2] 4 times; 3 dc in the beginning sp; ch 1, sc in the beginning dc *(this equals ch 2)*.

RND 3: Continuing with B, ch 3, 3 dc in the beginning sp; ch 4, skip the next ch-2 sp; [(4 dc, ch 2, 4 dc) in the next ch-2 sp; ch 4, skip the next ch-2 sp] 4 times; 4 dc in the beginning sp; ch 2, sl st in the 3rd ch of the beginning ch. Fasten off B.

All Sizes Carina Oct Centers (Make 2)

With A, ch 6; sl st in the beginning ch to form a ring.

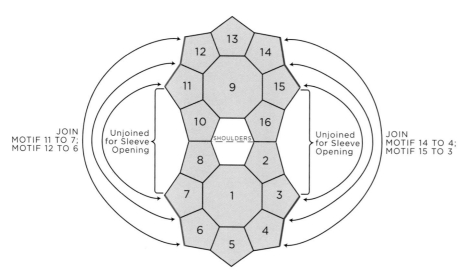

ASSEMBLY DIAGRAM SIZE XS/S AND M/L

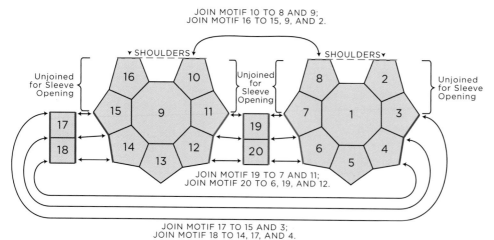

ASSEMBLY DIAGRAM SIZE L/XL

RND 1: Continuing with A, ch 3 *(this equals dc)*, 15 dc in the ring; sl st in the 3rd ch of the beginning ch—16 dc.

RND 2: Continuing with A, ch 4 *(this equals tr)*; 2 tr in the first dc; [ch 3, skip the next dc, 3 tr in the next dc] 7 times; ch 3, sl st in the 4th ch of the beginning chain. Fasten off A—8 ch-3 sps.

RND 3: With B, (air dc, 2 dc) in any ch-3 sp of Rnd 2; [ch 4, (3 dc, ch 2, 3 dc) in the next ch-3 sp] 7 times; ch 4, 3 dc in the beginning sp; ch 1, sc in the beginning dc *(this equals ch 2)*.

RND 4: Continuing with B, ch 3, 2 dc in the beginning sp; ch 4, skip the next ch-4 sp; [(3 dc, ch 2, 3 dc) in the next ch-2 sp; ch 4, skip the next ch-4 sp] 7 times; 3 dc in the beginning sp; ch 1, sc in the 3rd ch of the beginning ch.

RND 5: Continuing with B, ch 3, 3 dc in the beginning sp; ch 5, skip the next ch-4 sp; [(4 dc, ch 2, 4 dc) in the next ch-2 sp; ch 5, skip the next ch-4 sp] 7 times; 4 dc in the beginning sp; ch 2, sl st in the 3rd ch of the beginning ch. Fasten off B.

Carina Square Centers (for size XL/2XL gussets only) (Make 4)

With A, ch 4; sl st in the first ch to form a ring.

RND 1: Continuing with A, ch 6 *(this equals dc, ch 3)*, [dc in the ring, ch 3] 7 times; sl st in the 3rd ch of the beginning chain. Fasten off A—8 ch-3 sps.

RND 2: With B, (air dc, 3 dc) in any ch-3 sp of Rnd 1; ch 2, [skip the next ch-3 sp, (4 dc, ch 2, 4 dc) in the next ch-3 sp, ch 2] 3 times; 4 dc in the beginning sp; ch 2, sl st in the beginning dc. Fasten off B.

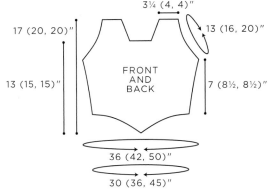

Assembly

Using MC, complete the motifs, connecting as you go while crocheting the last round of each motif according to the assembly diagram.

Size XS/S Assembly

The motifs in this size are finished as Carina minor class.

FRONT

MOTIF 1 (OCT): With MC, air sc in any ch-2 sp of Rnd 5 of one oct center; work Rnds 6–7 complete.

MOTIFS 2–8: With MC, air sc in any ch-2 sp of Rnd 3 of one pent center; work Rnd 4, then continue with Rnd 5, connecting completely to Motif 1 and to one another.

BACK

MOTIF 9 (OCT): Complete in same way as Motif 1.

MOTIFS 10–16: With MC, air sc in any ch-2 sp of Rnd 3 of one pent center; work Rnd 4, then continue with Rnd 5. Assemble each pent in the same way as Zodiac Motifs 10–16 (page 82), connecting the motifs at the shoulders and sides of the body.

Size M/L Assembly

The motifs in this size are finished as Carina major motifs.

FRONT

MOTIF 1 (OCT): With MC, air sc in any ch-2 sp of Rnd 5 of one oct center; work Rnds 6–8 complete.

MOTIFS 2–8: With MC, air sc in any ch-2 sp of Rnd 3 of one pent center; work Rnds 4–5, then continue with Rnd 6, connecting completely to Motif 1 oct and to one another.

BACK

MOTIF 9 (OCT): Complete in the same way as Motif 1 oct.

MOTIFS 10–16: With MC, air sc in any ch-2 sp of Rnd 3 of one pent center; work Rnds 4–5, then continue with Rnd 6. Assemble each pent in same way as Zodiac Motifs 10–16 (page 82), connecting the motifs at the tops of the shoulders and sides of the body.

Size XL/2XL Assembly

The motifs in this size are finished as Carina major motifs.

FRONT

MOTIF 1 (OCT): With MC, air sc in any ch-2 sp of Rnd 5 of one oct center; work Rnds 6–8 complete.

MOTIFS 2–8: With MC, air sc in any ch-2 sp of Rnd 3 of one pent center; work Rnds 4–5, then continue with Rnd 6, connecting completely to Motif 1 and to one another.

BACK

Unlike the smaller Callisto sizes and Zodiac, the back of this size is connected to the front at the top of the shoulders only.

MOTIF 9 (BODY OCT): Complete in same way as Motif 1.

MOTIF 10: Connect completely to the upper edge of Motif 8 *(at the shoulder line)*. Work the next 2 (3) side sps unattached, then connect completely to Motif 9. Finish the rest of the motif.

MOTIFS 11–15: Connect completely to the previous motif and to the next side of Motif 9, then finish the rest of the motif.

MOTIF 16: Connect completely to Motif 15 and to the next side of Motif 9. Work the next 2 (3) side sps unattached, then connect completely to the upper edge of Motif 2 *(at the shoulder line)*. Finish the rest of the motif.

SIDE GUSSETS

Mark the point joins between Motifs 3 and 4, between Motifs 6 and 7, between Motifs 11 and 12, and between Motifs 14 and 15. With the right side of the pieces facing, insert two squares at each side of the body, connecting to the side edges of the Front and Back and to one another.

With MC, air sc in any ch-2 sp of Rnd 2 of a square center; work Rnds 3–4, then continue with Rnd 5, connecting as you go.

MOTIF 17: Join the first point sp to the marked join between Motifs 14 and 15; connect the next 3 side sps and the next point sp to Motif 15. Work the next 3 side sps unattached *(for the underarm)*. Folding at the shoulder line to make this next bit easier, join the next point sp to the free point sp of Motif 3, then connect the next 3 side spaces to Motif 3. Join the next point sp to the marked join between Motifs 3 and 4, and finish the rest of the motif.

MOTIF 18: Join the first point sp to the free point sp of Motif 14, then connect the next 3 side sps to Motif 14. Join the next point sp to the marked join between Motifs 14 and 15, then connect the next 3 side sps to Motif 17. Join the next point sp to the join between Motifs 3 and 4, then connect the next 3 side sps and the next point sp to Motif 4; finish the rest of the motif.

MOTIF 19: Join the first point sp to the marked join between Motifs 6 and 7, then connect the next 3 side sps and the next point sp to Motif 7. Work the next 3 side sps unattached *(for the underarm)*. Folding at shoulder line to make this next bit easier, join the next point sp to the free point sp of Motif 11, then connect the next 3 side sps to Motif 11. Join the next point sp to the marked join between Motifs 11 and 12, and finish the rest of the motif.

MOTIF 20: Join the first point sp to the free point sp of Motif 6, then connect next 3 side sps to Motif 6. Join the next point sp to the marked join between Motifs 6 and 7, then connect the next 3 side sps to Motif 19. Join the next point sp to the join between Motifs 11 and 12, then connect the next 3 side sps and the next point sp to Motif 12; finish the rest of the motif.

At this fine gauge, the neck, armhole, and bottom edges of Callisto are left unbound to offer more stretch, plus on/off ease. Weave in the ends, and block.

phoebe SHRUG

Stripped down to just a handful of pentagons, this construction creates the tiniest shoulder-hugging shrug. The ribbed trim helps keep the motif edges snug against the body and makes Phoebe upside-downable. Yes, it's complicated, but so very cute (and quick) that you might find yourself making more than one.

skill level
EXPERIENCED ● ● ●

Size
XS/S (M/L); sample shown is size XS/S

Finished width at underarm 20 (23)" (51 [58.5] cm); length, total at center back 11½ (13½)" (29.5 [34.5]cm)

Materials
Misti Alpaca Tonos Pima Silk, 83% pima cotton, 17% silk, 3½ oz (100g), 327 yd (300m) **2** Fine

1 (2) hanks in TPS11 Berry Rich

U.S. Size 7 (4.5mm) crochet hook or size needed to obtain gauge

Stitch markers

Gauge
In ribbing of band, 16 hdc = 4" (10cm); 6 rows = 2" (5cm)

For Size XS/S

Carina Minor Pent Motif
RND 1: 1½" (3.8cm)

RND 2: 2¾" (7cm) widest point

RND 5: one side, point to point = 3½" (9cm); height = 6" (15cm); widest point = 6½" (16.5cm)

For Size M/L

Carina Major Pent Motif
RND 1: 1½" (3.8cm)

RND 2: 2¾" (7cm) widest point

RND 6: one side, point to point = 4½" (11.5cm); height = 7" (18cm); widest point = 7½" (19cm)

Please see Measuring Motifs (page 35).

Stitch Definitions
See instructions for individual Carina motifs (page 25).

For more motif assembly information, see Universal Assembly (page 33).

Pattern Notes
I rarely approve of how variegated yarns behave in lace crochet or in lacy motifs. High-contrast color changes can detract from your lovely stitchwork. However, many tonal yarns, those with subtly shifting shades throughout a related range of colors, can bring breathtaking depth to lace. This yarn is particularly noteworthy for the way in which the silk and cotton take on color so brilliantly.

Working with Half Double Crochet (hdc) Ribbing

For a beautiful ribbed texture but very little compression, I love half double crochet made in the front loop only (hdc through the front loop only). The wrong side of hdc has a unique feature among standard crochet stitches, an extra horizontal strand that lies below the top loops of the stitch. The front loop of the half double crochet is the strand on top of the row, *not* this extra strand just below.

HDC THROUGH THE FRONT LOOP ONLY: YO, insert the hook in the front loop only of the next stitch, YO and draw up a loop, YO and draw through all 3 loops on the hook.

BEG HDC: Begin a row of hdc with an actual stitch in the first hdc, a stitch that is linked to the ch-2 turning chain. Ch 2, insert the hook in the 2nd ch from the hook, YO and draw up a loop, insert the hook in the first hdc, YO and draw up a loop, YO and draw through all 3 loops on the hook.

Instructions

Size XS/S uses Carina minor pents.

Size M/L uses Carina major pents.

The first 8 motifs are assembled in a curved course. But there are two odd connections between the outer points of Motifs 4 and 1, and between the outer points of Motifs 5 and 8.

Make 11 Carina pent motifs, connecting to one another as you go while crocheting the last round according to the assembly diagram.

MOTIFS 1–3: Assemble 3 pents in a curved row, connected completely to one another, with one flat side of each at the inside of curve and a free point of each at the outer curve.

MOTIF 4: Add to the curved assembly the same as previous motifs, except join the outer point sp to the free outer point sp of Motif 1. Fold over Motif 3 at the shoulder line to make this possible.

MOTIFS 5–7: Add to the curved assembly the same as previous motifs.

MOTIF 8: Add to the curved assembly the same as previous motifs, except join the outer point sp to the free outer point sp of Motif 5. Fold over Motif 6 at the shoulder line to make this possible.

MOTIF 9: Join the first point sp to the outer free point sp of Motif 3; connect the next 2 (3) side sps to Motif 3. Join the next point sp to the join between Motifs 3 and 4, then con-nect the next 2 (3) side sps to Motif 4. Join the next point sp to the join between Motifs 1 and 4, and then connect the next 2 (3) side sps to Motif 1. Join the next point sp to the join between Motifs 1 and 2, and then connect the next 2 (3) side sps to Motif 2. Join the last point sp to the outer free point sp of Motif 2. Finish the rest of the motif.

MOTIF 10: Join first point sp to the outer free point sp of Motif 7, then connect the next 2 (3) side sps to Motif 7. Join the next point sp to the join between Motifs 7 and 8, then connect the next 2 (3) side sps to Motif 8. Join the next point sp to the join between Motifs 5 and 8, then connect the next 2 (3) side sps to Motif 5. Join the next point sp to the join between Motifs 5 and 6, then connect the next 2 (3) side sps to Motif 6. Join the last point sp to the outer free point sp of Motif 6, and finish the rest of the motif.

MOTIF 11: Join the first point sp to the next free point sp of Motif 1, then connect the next 2 (3) side sps to Motif 1. Join the next point sp to the join between Motifs 1 and 4 *(yes,*

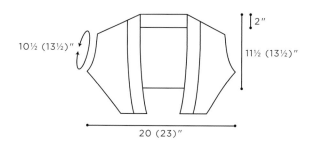

ASSEMBLY DIAGRAM

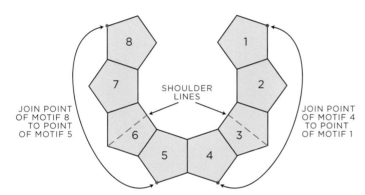

JOIN POINT
OF MOTIF 8
TO POINT
OF MOTIF 5

SHOULDER
LINES

JOIN POINT
OF MOTIF 4
TO POINT
OF MOTIF 1

WHILE JOINING MOTIFS 1 THROUGH 8
IN A SEMICIRCLE AS SHOWN,
JOIN AT POINTS AS INDICATED

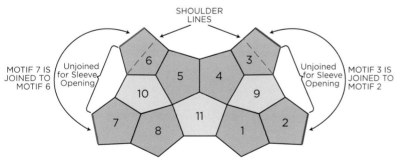

SHOULDER
LINES

MOTIF 7 IS
JOINED TO
MOTIF 6

Unjoined
for Sleeve
Opening

Unjoined
for Sleeve
Opening

MOTIF 3 IS
JOINED TO
MOTIF 2

JOIN MOTIF 9 TO 3, 4, 1, AND 2;
JOIN MOTIF 10 TO 7, 8, 5, AND 6;
JOIN MOTIF 11 TO 1, 4, 5, AND 8

there are four points here), then connect the next 2 (3) side sps to Motif 4. Join the next point sp to the join between Motifs 4 and 5, then connect the next 2 (3) side sps to Motif 5. Join the next point sp to the join between Motifs 5 and 8, then connect the next 2 (3) side sps to Motif 8. Join the last point sp to the next free point sp of Motif 8, and finish the rest of the motif.

Band

Finish the inner curve of the front neckline (the one flat side each of Motifs 1–8) and add a wide band.

With the right side of the front edge facing, join yarn with sl st in the remaining free point sp of Motif 8 at one end of the inner curve.

ROW 1 (RS): Ch 1, [sc, ch 4, sc] in the same sp; *[ch 4, sc in the next ch-4 sp] 2 (3) times; ch 4, sc in the next partial ch-sp before the join of the motifs; ch 4, sc in the next partial ch-sp after the join of motifs*; repeat from * to * 6 times; [ch 4, sc in next ch-4 sp] 2 (3) times; ch 4, (sc, ch 4, sc) in the next ch-4 sp *(the remaining free point sp of Motif 1);* turn—32 (40) ch-4 sps.

ROW 2 (WS): Beg hdc in the first sc; 4 hdc in each ch-4 sp across; hdc in the last sc; turn—130 (162) hdc.

ROW 3: Beg hdc, hdc through the front loop only in each stitch to the last stitch; hdc in both loops of the last hdc; turn.

ROWS 4-7: Repeat Row 3 4 times, then fasten off.

Weave in the ends, and block.

angular momentum

With so much crazy lace-motif assembly going on, it's essential to draft a good old reliable stitch pattern to do the grunt work. With its angled extended shells (Eshells) and staggered chain spaces, Angular Momentum adapts to interior shaping, carries through many of the themes of the spawn of Entropy, and integrates seamlessly with headers and motif edges.

The original Entropy doily offers one more plaything, the expanding Corsair stitch figure. Working back and forth in rows, you can create a curved section that has many applications. Angular Momentum and Corsair appear separately and also orbit in tandem.

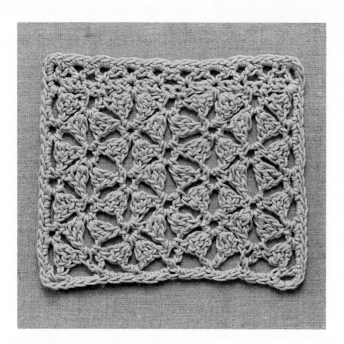

Angular Momentum Stitch Pattern

Angular Momentum plays a role in the designs in this chapter. The same stitch pattern worked in connected rounds is used in the Tempest Skirt and Poncho (page 16).

Stitch Definitions

EDC (EXTENDED DOUBLE CROCHET): YO, insert the hook in the stitch or sp indicated, YO and draw up a loop, YO and draw through one loop on the hook (as if to ch 1); [YO and draw through the 2 loops on the hook] 2 times.

ESHELL (EXTENDED DC-DC-DC SHELL): *This is a 3-stitch shell with an edc as the first arm, then two dc made in the ch at the base of the edc.*

Edc in the st or sp indicated; YO, insert hook in the ch at the base of the edc just made, *YO and draw up a loop; [YO and draw through 2 loops on the hook] 2 times*; YO, insert the hook in the same ch at the base of the edc; repeat from * to * for the second dc.

FAN (USED TO INCREASE 2 CH-3 SPS AT A CORNER): [Dc, (ch 3, dc) 3 times] all in the same sp as indicated.

Stitch Pattern Rows

Plug in these two Pattern Rows when directed to work even (without increases or decreases):

PATTERN ROW A: Ch 4 *(this equals dc, ch 1)*, sc in the beginning ch-sp; [(Eshell, ch 3, Eshell) in the next ch-3 sp, (sc, ch 3, sc) in the next ch-3 sp] across to the last ch-3 sp; (Eshell, ch 3, Eshell) in the last ch-3 sp; (sc, ch 1, dc) in the tch sp; turn.

PATTERN ROW B: Ch 5 *(this equals tr, ch 1)*, Eshell in the beginning ch-sp; [sc, ch 3, sc] in the next ch-3 sp; [(Eshell, ch 3, Eshell) in the next ch-3 sp, (sc, ch 3, sc) in the next ch-3 sp] across; (Eshell, ch 1, tr) in tch sp; turn.

Working with Angular Momentum

STARTING

Generally speaking, Angular Momentum is a stitch pattern equal to nine stitches in gauge. In other words, to start the pattern on a foundation and have it be completely flat and straight at the beginning edge, you would use nine foundation stitches per repeat. The stitch diagram below shows how this would work, as used in the designs T-Bird Four Ways (page 106), Fairlane Jacket (page 109), and Eldorado Jacket (page 113). But Angular Momentum is flexible enough to start on fewer foundation stitches to get a jump start on curved shaping. Tempest (page 16) uses eight stitches of foundation per repeat for a smooth transition to shoulder/hip shaping.

MEASURING

To measure gauge, stretch the fabric in all directions, smoothing it out—but let it snap back if it wants to. For stitch gauge, measure from between the feet (bottom of the stems) of 2 Eshells to between the feet of the next 2 shells. For row gauge over 4 rows, begin measuring from the feet of 2 Eshells, skip the next Eshells directly above, and end at the feet of the next Eshells above.

COUNTING

Notice how the repeats of this stitch pattern can be counted. This is a shifting pattern, so if you try to count the "points" you won't have the same number of whole points every row. Often I will give Angular Momentum counts in terms of ch-3 sps, which remain constant while the stitch pattern is worked even, without increases or decreases.

INCREASING

The pattern always follows the same progression except for rows that increase. In an increase row, instead of (Eshell, ch 3, Eshell) in a corner ch-3 sp according to the progression, work a fan in each corner ch-3 sp. The fan adds a ch-3 sp before and after each corner ch-3 sp.

In the row that follows, treat the ch-3 sps of the fan the same as the other ch-3 sps, and return to the regular pattern progression across the corners. In other words, (sc, ch 3, sc) in the first ch-3 sp of the fan, (Eshell, ch 3, Eshell) in the 2nd ch-3 sp of the fan, (sc, ch 3, sc) in the third ch-3 sp of the fan. Remember to move or wrap markers up into the ch-3 sp at the center of each corner as you go.

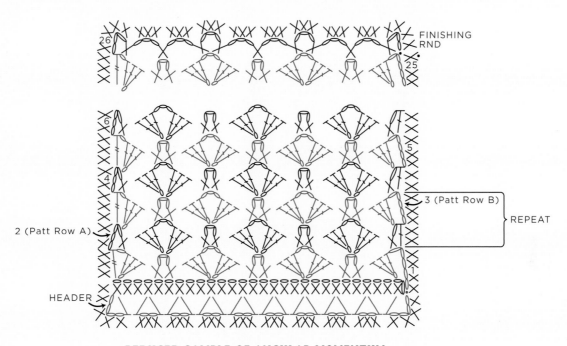

REDUCED SAMPLE OF ANGULAR MOMENTUM STITCH PATTERN

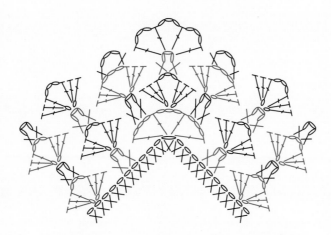

ANGULAR MOMENTUM INCREASE PATTERN

corsair COLLAR

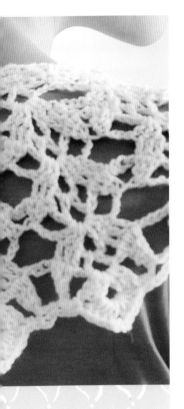

The Corsair stitch figure is a stack of sprays, either leaves or wings depending on how you look at it. The nature of Corsair is to radiate outward and expand as it goes along, so it is the perfect stitch pattern for adding an automatic flare or ruffle to a garment. Corsair puts the flirt in T-Bird Four Ways.

I am a no-frills kind of girl, opting out of most decorative doodads. But I couldn't resist designing this detachable collar, a romantic touch when strung to a neckline header, as shown with Fairlane Jacket (page 109). You may also string Corsair and wear it separately as a ruffled scarf, or not string it and let it cascade freely around the shoulders with perhaps a button accent. Try crocheting the same pattern in an exploded gauge and thicker yarn for a longer, wider stole; thread the header of a Corsair stole on a café rod to hang as a window valence.

skill level
EXPERIENCED ● ● ●

Size
Adjustable
Finished length, header 26″ (66cm); total depth 6½″ (16.5cm)

Materials
Spud & Chloë Fine, 80% superwash wool, 20% silk, 2¼ oz (65g), 248 yd (227m) **1** Super Fine
One hank in #7800 Popcorn, or approximately 230 yd (212m) sock/fingering weight yarn
U.S. Size G-6 (4mm) crochet hook or size needed to obtain gauge

Gauge
17 fsc = 4″ (10cm)

Stitch Definitions
FSC (FOUNDATION SINGLE CROCHET): See Chainless Foundations (page 140).

DC3TOG CLUSTER (DOUBLE CROCHET 3 TOGETHER IN DIFFERENT PLACES): [YO, insert the hook into the next stitch indicated, YO and draw up a loop, YO and draw through the 2 loops on the hook] 3 times; YO and draw through all 4 loops on the hook.

TR3TOG CLUSTER (TRIPLE CROCHET 3 TOGETHER IN DIFFERENT PLACES): *YO 2 times, insert the hook in the next stitch indicated, YO and draw up a loop, [YO and draw through the 2 loops on the hook] 2 times*; repeat from * to * 2 times, YO and draw through all 4 loops on the hook.

Pattern Notes
The Corsair stitch figure begins on a foundation that is a multiple of 6 foundation single crochet stitches plus one extra for the edge stitch. To create a longer or shorter piece, adjust the foundation by adding or omitting multiples of 6 fsc.

Instructions

Fsc 109 to measure 26″ (66cm); turn the foundation over so the sc edge is on top, then begin working across the sc edge, making the header first.

HEADER (RS): Ch 4, hdc in the first sc; [skip the next 2 sc, (hdc, ch 2, hdc) in the next sc] 35 times; skip next 2 sc; (hdc, ch 4, sl st) in the last sc; do not turn—37 ch-sps.

Rotate the foundation so the chain edge is on top, begin working across the chain edge.

ROW 1 (RS): Ch 4 *(this equals dc, ch 1)*, dc in the first ch; [[ch 2, skip next 2 chains, sc in the next ch, ch 2, skip the next 2 chs, (dc, ch 3, dc) in the next ch] 17 times; ch 2, skip the next 2 chains, sc in the next ch; ch 2, skip the next 2 chains, (dc, ch 1, dc) in the last ch; turn—18 Corsair repeats (17 points plus half points at ends).

ROW 2: Ch 5 *(this equals tr, ch 1)*, 3 dc in the beginning sp; [ch 3, skip next 2 ch-2 sp, (3 dc, ch 4, 3 dc) in the next ch-3 sp] 17 times; ch 3, skip the next 2 ch-2 sps, (3 dc, ch 1, tr) in the turning chain space; turn.

ROW 3: Ch 4, dc in the beginning sp; *ch 2, dc in each of the next 3 dc stitches; ch 2, skip the next ch-3 sp, dc in each of the next 3 dc stitches; ch 2**, (dc, ch 3, dc) in the next ch-4 sp*; repeat from * to * 16 times, then repeat from * to **; (dc, ch 1, dc) in the turning chain space; turn.

NOTE: *The following six rows (Rows 4–9) are used in the designs T-Bird (page 106) and Andromeda Peplum Vest (page 129).*

ROW 4: Ch 5, 3 dc in the beginning sp; *ch 3, skip the next ch-2 sp, dc3tog cluster in the next 3 dc stitches, skip the next ch-2 sp, dc3tog cluster in the next 3 dc stitches; ch 3, skip the next ch-2 sp**, (3 dc, ch 4, 3 dc) in the next ch-3 sp*; repeat from * to * 16 times, then repeat from * to **; end with (3 dc, ch 1, tr) in the turning chain space; turn.

ROW 5: Ch 4, dc in the beginning sp; *ch 2, dc in each of the next 3 dc stitches; ch 3, skip the next 2 clusters, dc in each of the next 3 dc stitches; ch 2**, (dc, ch 3, dc) in the next ch-4 sp*; repeat from * to * 16 times, then repeat from * to **; (dc, ch 1, dc) in the turning chain space; turn.

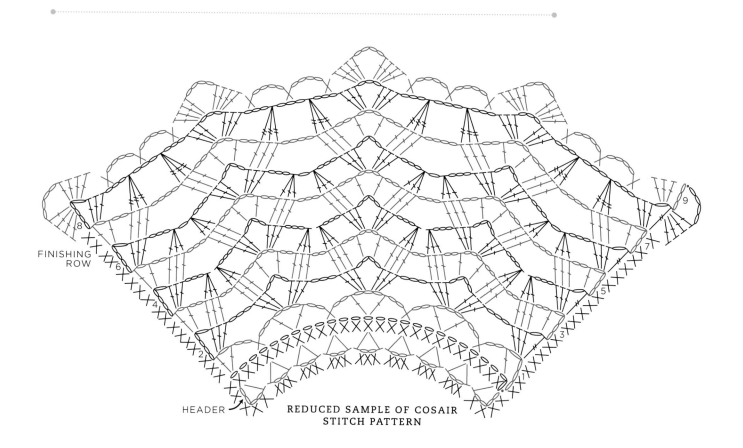

FINISHING ROW

HEADER   REDUCED SAMPLE OF COSAIR
STITCH PATTERN

ROW 6: Ch 5, 3 dc in the beginning sp; *ch 3, skip the next ch-2 sp, dc3tog cluster in the next 3 dc stitches; ch 1, skip the next ch-3 sp, dc3tog cluster in the next 3 dc stitches; ch 3, skip the next ch-2 sp**; (3 dc, ch 4, 3 dc) in the next ch-3 sp*; repeat from * to * 16 times, then repeat from * to **; (3 dc, ch 1, tr) in the turning chain space; turn.

ROW 7: Ch 4, dc in the beginning sp; *ch 2, dc in each of the next 3 dc stitches; ch 4, skip the next 2 clusters, dc in each of the next 3 dc stitches; ch 2**, (dc, ch 3, dc) in the next ch-4 sp*; repeat from * to * 16 times, then repeat from * to **; (dc, ch 1, dc) in the turning chain space; turn.

ROW 8: Ch 5, 3 dc in the beginning sp; *ch 3, skip the next ch-2 sp, tr3tog cluster in the next 3 dc stitches; ch 3, skip the next ch-4 sp, tr3tog cluster in the next 3 dc stitches; ch 3, skip the next ch-2 sp**, (3 dc, ch 3, 3 dc) in the next ch-3 sp*; repeat from * to * 16 times, then repeat from * to **; (3 dc, ch 1, tr) in the turning chain space; turn.

ROW 9: Ch 3 *(this equals dc)*, 3 dc in the beginning sp; *(no ch-4 here)* sc in the next ch-3 sp; [ch 4, sc in the next ch-3 sp] 2 times; *(no ch-4 here)* **(4 dc, ch 4, 4 dc) in the next ch-3 sp*; repeat from * to * 16 times, then repeat from * to **; (4 dc, ch 4, 4 dc) in the turning chain space; do not turn.

Rotate and continue to work the edging across the row edges of the two short sides and across the header.

FINISHING RND (RS): [2 sc in the next dc row edge, 3 sc in the next tr row edge] 3 times; 2 sc in the next dc row edge, sc in the Fsc row edge; 4 sc in the beginning ch-4 sp of the header; 3 sc in each of the next 35 ch-2 sps of the header; 4 sc in the last sp of the header; sc in the Fsc row edge, [2 sc in the next dc row edge, 3 sc in the next tr row edge] 3 times; 2 sc in the next dc row edge; 4 dc in the next tr row edge; ch 4, sl st in the 3rd ch of the beginning ch. Fasten off.

Weave in the ends and block into an arc, roughly two-thirds of a round.

Choose a string type (page 137) as desired. Make one string 45" (114cm) long or to taste.

Make optional button (page 138) as desired.

t-bird

t-bird FOUR WAYS

One long special rectangle leads many lives. Draped here, or gathered and tucked there, or captured with string and a few buttons, T-Bird transforms from a stole to a skirted sari wrap to a ruffled cardi.

T-Bird features three elements that combine to make magic. The header is the key to the transformability, Angular Momentum provides the basic fabric, and Corsair gives the edge a flirty finish.

skill level

EASY   ● ○ ○

Size
68" (172.5cm) by 19" (48.5cm)

Materials
NaturallyCaron.com Spa, 75% microdenier acrylic, 25% rayon from bamboo, 3 oz (85g), 251 yd (230m) **(3)** Light

5 skeins in 0012 Black, or approximately 1,100 yd (1,006m) sport weight yarn

U.S. Size H-8 (5mm) crochet hook or size needed to obtain gauge

Also needed for Cardi styling:
Stitch markers
16" (40.5cm) button bridge (page 138)
¾" (20mm) button studs (page 140)

Gauge
16 fsc or sc = 4" (10cm)

In Angular Momentum stitch pattern, one repeat = 2¼" (5.5cm); 4 rows = 2½" (6.5cm)

Stitch Definitions
FSC (FOUNDATION SINGLE CROCHET): See Chainless Foundations (page 140).

See Angular Momentum Stitch Pattern (page 98) for stitches and pattern rows.

See Corsair (page 101) for stitches and pattern rows.

Instructions

Fsc 271 to measure approximately 68" (172.5cm). Turn the foundation over so the sc edge is on top, then begin work across sc edge.

HEADER: Ch 4, hdc in first sc; [skip next 2 sc, (hdc, ch 2, hdc) in next sc] 89 times; skip next 2 sc, (hdc, ch 4, sl st) in the last sc; do not turn.

Rotate the foundation so the chain edge is on top, then begin to work across the chain edge. Using 9 stitches of foundation per repeat, set up 30 repeats of Angular Momentum stitch pattern.

ROW 1: Ch 5, Eshell in the first ch, skip the next 3 chs, sc in the next ch; ch 3, sc in the next ch, skip the next 3 chs, [(Eshell, ch 3, Eshell) in the next ch, skip the next 3 chs, sc in the next ch; ch 3, sc in the next ch, skip the next 3 chs] 29 times; (Eshell, ch 1, tr) in the last ch; turn—59 ch-3 sps (29 points plus half points at ends).

ROW 2 (PATTERN ROW A): Ch 4 *(this equals dc, ch 1)*, sc in the beginning ch-sp; [(Eshell, ch 3, Eshell) in the next ch-3 sp; (sc, ch 3, sc) in the next ch-3 sp] across to the last ch-3 sp; (Eshell, ch 3, Eshell) in the last ch-3 sp; (sc, ch 1, dc) in the turning chain space; turn.

ROW 3 (PATTERN ROW B): Ch 5 *(this equals tr, ch 1)*, Eshell in the beginning ch-sp, (sc, ch 3, sc) in the next ch-3 sp; [(Eshell, ch 3, Eshell) in the next ch-3 sp; (sc, ch 3, sc) in the next ch-3 sp] across; (Eshell, ch 1, tr) in the turning chain space; turn.

ROWS 4–19: Work Angular Momentum [Pattern Row A, Pattern Row B] (page 98) 8 times.

For a lacy flounced edge, add the slightly ruffling Corsair Stitch Pattern rows (page 102).

ROW 20: Ch 4, dc in the beginning sp; *ch 2, dc in each of the next 3 dc stitches; ch 2, skip the next ch-3 sp *(between the sc)*, dc in each of next 3 dc stiches; ch 2**, (dc, ch 3, dc) in the next ch-3 sp *(between Eshells)**; repeat from * to * 28 times, then repeat from * to **; (dc, ch 1, dc) in the turning chain space; turn—30 Corsair repeats (29 points plus half points at ends).

ROWS 21–26: Work in the same way as Corsair Collar (page 102) Rows 4–9 across 30 repeats.

Finishing

Rotate and continue to work a finishing row of sc across the row edges of the two short sides and across the header.

FINISHING RND: [2 sc in the next dc row edge, 3 sc in the next tr row edge] 12 times; sc in the Fsc row edge, 5 sc in the beginning ch-4 sp of the header; 3 sc in each of the next 89 ch-2 sps of the header; 5 sc in the last ch-4 sp of the header; sc in the Fsc row edge, [3 sc in the next tr row edge, 2 sc in the next dc row edge] 12 times; 4 dc in the last tr row edge; ch 4, sl st in the 3rd ch of the beginning ch. Fasten off.

Weave in the ends, and block.

Buttons

T-Bird doesn't need closures to style as a stole or sari wrap.

FOR CARDI ASSEMBLY AS SHOWN: Make a button bridge to 16″ (40.5cm) total length and 6 button studs.

Ⓐ Styling the Sari Wrap

Start with the rectangle in front of you. For a wrap that covers the left shoulder, begin at the right hip; for a wrap that covers the right shoulder, begin at the left hip. Hold one end at your side, tucking the header into your clothing waistband or a belt. Keeping hold of the tuck so it doesn't come out, wrap the T-Bird across your front, around the other side of body and across your back until it meets the tuck. Overlapping and covering the tuck, bring the stole up from your hip, cross your heart to the opposite shoulder from the tuck, toss the end of the stole over your shoulder from front to back. Adjust all around until it looks good.

Ⓒ Styling the Cardi

The Cardi uses a button bridge (page 138) to thread the header to itself at the back and portion out two armholes. You will need at least two button studs (page 140), plus as many more studs as desired, plus two safety pins or stitch markers.

Locate and mark the hdc V at dead center of the header. Lay the T-Bird flat on a table in front of you, with the right side facing and the header below. Curve the ends of the stole down and around so that the two ends of the header meet in the middle of a circle of fabric. With a second marker, pin the two ends of the header together through the first ch-sp holes at each edge, temporarily joining the two edge stitches. The piece will resemble an oval and be rather crumpled in the middle.

Match the markers. Take one loop end of the button bridge, bring the loop from back to front up through the ch-sp hole of the center back V, up through the ch-sp hole at one end of the header, over the marked edge stitches, down the ch-sp hole at the other side of the marker, and down through the same hole of the center back V. Slide the bridge through so it's even on both sides of this center spot.

Matching ch-sp holes of the Vs across, threading through both thicknesses, [weave one loop end up through the ch-sp hole of the next V from back to front, then down through the ch-sp hole of the next V from front to back] 4 times, then up through the ch-sp hole of the next V. Slip one button stud through both thicknesses in the ch-sp hole of the next V, then slip the bridge loop over the button to secure this end. Return to the other end of the bridge, weave in and out of both thicknesses of header in the other direction and secure with a button stud in the same way. Use additional studs to close the edges of the cardi down the center back as desired.

fairlane JACKET

Add one shallow angle to the center back and you've got a V-shaped wrap that stays on your shoulders. Crocheted in a comfortable and comforting blend of organic wool and cotton, this is a season-spanning layer you'll want to live in. The edges of Angular Momentum offer regularly spaced button loops that can be used to convert Fairlane into a front-angled jacket. The header may be used to thread stuff, too, as shown on page 103 with a Corsair Collar.

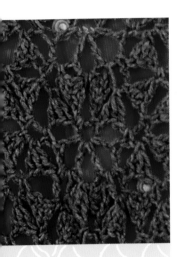

skill level
EASY ● ○ ○

Size
Finished width, one front 17" (43cm); length, one front from center back neck 25" (63.5cm); depth, back neck to point 23" (58.5cm)

Materials
O-Wool Balance, 50% certified organic merino wool, 50% certified organic cotton, 1¾ oz (50g), 130 yd (120m) (4) Medium

7 hanks in #3222 Malachite

U.S. Size I-9 (5.5mm) crochet hook or size needed to obtain gauge

Stitch markers

¾" (20mm) button studs (page 140, optional)

Corsair Collar (page 101, optional)

Gauge
13 fsc or sc = 4" (10cm)

In Angular Momentum Stitch Pattern, one repeat = 2¾" (7cm); 4 rows = 3" (7.5cm) as crocheted. Blocking will alter the finished fabric—as the fibers soften and bulk up, the row gauge shrinks (!) to 4 rows = 2¾" (7cm).

Stitch Definitions
FSC (FOUNDATION SINGLE CROCHET): See Chainless Foundations (page 140).

See Angular Momentum Stitch Pattern (page 98) for stitches and pattern rows.

Instructions

Fsc 163 to measure approximately 50″ (127cm). Turn the foundation over so sc edge is on top, then begin to work across the sc edge.

HEADER: Ch 4 *(this equals [hdc, ch 2])*, hdc in the first sc, [skip the next 2 sc, (hdc, ch 2, hdc) in the next sc] 53 times; skip the next 2 sc, (hdc, ch 4, sl st) in the last sc. Do not turn.

Rotate the foundation so the chain edge is on top. Begin work across the chain edge.

ROW 1: Ch 5, Eshell in the first ch; skip the next 3 chs, sc in the next ch; ch 3, sc in the next ch; skip the next 3 chs, [(Eshell, ch 3, Eshell) in the next ch, skip the next 3 chs, sc in the next ch; ch 3, sc in the next ch, skip the next 3 chs] 8 times. Work a fan in the next ch; skip the next 3 chs, sc in the next ch; ch 3, sc in the next ch, skip the next 3 chs; repeat between [ ] 8 times; (Eshell, ch 1, tr) in the last ch; turn—37 ch-3 sps.

Mark the middle (second) ch-3 sp of the fan at center back, and move or wrap the marker up as you go into the ch-3 sp at the center of the angle.

Maintaining the ends of the rows in the Angular Momentum sequence [Pattern Row A, Pattern Row B], work a fan at the center back marker of every third row.

ROW 2: Work Pattern Row A.

ROW 3: Work Pattern Row B.

ROW 4: Begin as Pattern Row A, work in the pattern as established to the next marked ch-3 sp of the angle at the center back; work a fan in the marked ch-3 sp, then complete the row in the pattern as established; end as Pattern Row A—39 ch-3 sps.

ROW 5: Work Pattern Row B.

ROW 6: Work Pattern Row A.

ROW 7: Begin as Pattern Row B, work in the pattern as established to the next marked ch-3 sp of the angle at the center back; work a fan in the marked ch-3 sp, then complete the row in the pattern as established; end as Pattern Row B—41 ch-3 sps.

ROWS 8–25: Repeat Rows 2–7 3 times—53 ch-3 sps.

ROW 26: Ch 3, sc in the beginning sp, [ch 3, sc in the next ch-3 sp; ch 3, (sc, ch 3, sc) in the next ch-3 sp] 26 times; ch 3, sc in the next ch-3 sp; ch 3, sc in the turning chain space; ch 3, sl st in the 4th ch of the turning chain; do not turn—82 ch-3 sps.

Finishing

Rotate and continue to work a finishing round of sc across all edges.

FINISHING RND: Ch 1, 3 sc in the next tr row edge; [2 sc in the next dc row edge, 3 sc in the next tr row edge] 12 times; sc in the foundation sc row edge, 4 sc in the beginning ch-4 sp of the header. Rotate the work, then 3 sc in each ch-2 sp across the header; 4 sc in the last ch-4 sp of the header. Rotate the work, then sc in the foundation sc row edge, 3 sc in the next tr row edge, [2 sc in the next dc row edge, 3 sc in the next tr row edge] 12 times. Rotate the work, then 3 sc in each ch-3 sp of Row 26; sl st in the beginning sc. Fasten off.

Weave in the ends, and block.

Button Studs (optional)

Fairlane is shown assembled into a jacket using button studs to connect the lower few inches at each side to the back point. O Wool Balance yarn is not sturdy enough for crocheted buttons, so the sample is shown using six pairs of ¾″ (20mm) purchased buttons.

Corsair Collar (optional)

Make the collar as written (page 101). Because the gauge of the collar is not the same as Fairlane, the header holes will not have the same spacing. Center the collar along the neck edge of the wrap. Beginning at the center back, thread one end of the string through both thicknesses of headers, going through two header Vs of the collar for every one header V of wrap to the end of the collar; do the other end of the string from the center back to end of the collar in the same way.

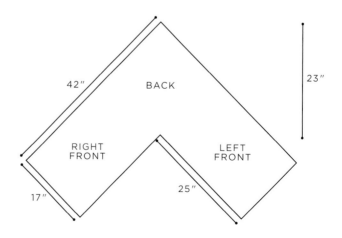

eldorado JACKET

For ultimate coziness, Eldorado is a wrap with ample coverage. Constructed with two angles at the back, Eldo is boomerang shaped and boxier in fit than Fairlane. Eldo becomes a blanket jacket with the optional long, squishy cuffs that can be folded up or left long to cover the hands, almost like fingerless mitts.

This sample illustrates a very cool and simple way to get the best out of this special hand-dyed yarn, which can vary greatly from hank to hank. The resulting interplay of shades is ever-changing and spectacular and the fabric brings out a geometry in Angular Momentum that you don't see when the stitch pattern is crocheted in one solid color.

skill level
EXPERIENCED ● ● ●

Size
Finished length, center back 24" (61cm); width, one front 22" (56cm)

Materials
Manos del Uruguay Rittenhouse Merino 5-ply, 100% pure extrafine merino wool kettle dyed, 3½ oz (100g), 240 yd (220m) Medium

4 hanks in 512 Cinnamon (semi-solid MC1, MC2); 2 hanks in 599 Agate (variegated CC)

U.S. Size J-10 (6mm) crochet hook or size needed to obtain gauge

Stitch markers

Gauge
12 fsc, sc, or hdc = 4" (10cm)

In Angular Momentum Stitch Pattern, one repeat = 3" (7.5cm); 4 rows = 3¼" (8cm)

In hdc blo ribbing of cuffs, 8 rows = 4" (10cm)

Stitch Definitions
FSC (FOUNDATION SINGLE CROCHET): See Chainless Foundations (page 140).

See Angular Momentum Stitch Pattern (page 98) for stitches and pattern rows.

See Phoebe Shrug (page 94) for more information about working with hdc ribbing.

Working with Color Changes

Normally you'd see this method used for working one row each in three colors without having to cut yarn at the end of every row. One unused strand is carried up each side of the row. Eldo does the exact same thing. Although there are just two different shades, a semi-solid tonal and a short repeat variegated, they are in a three-color scheme. For MC1 and MC2 use two separate feeds of the main color (semi-solid), each taken from different hanks the better to smooth out any drastic gradations in color; for CC use one feed of the coordinating variegated color.

The ends of rows are a constant parade of [Pattern Row A, Pattern Row B] no matter what is happening in the middle of the row, so managing the color changes at the ends is the same throughout. Keep track of the three feeds as you carry and wrap the strands at the end of every row, and reposition the yarn balls each time you turn the work to avoid a ginormous tangled mess.

TIP: *When stranding yarn up the side of the work, do it neatly but loosely. That way you will allow the edges as much elasticity as the rest of the stitch pattern. Resist the temptation to yank those feeds tightly!*

At the end of a row: *This stitch pattern ends with either a dc (Pattern Row A) or a triple crochet (Pattern Row B). Either way, for the last stitch, YO as required, insert the hook in the turning chain space, YO, and draw up a loop. *Pick up the ball of the next yarn from below, bring it from under the working yarn to the front, then wrap it from front to back, up and over the working yarn. With the working yarn, YO and draw through the 2 loops on the hook.* For a tr, repeat from * to *. Pick up the ball of the next yarn and wrap again. Now drop the working yarn, YO with the next yarn, and draw through the 2 loops on the hook to complete the final st of the row in new yarn. Don't turn yet.*

At the beginning of a row: *Rows begin with ch 4 (Pattern Row A) or ch 5 (Pattern Row B). Now wrap the old yarn in the turning chains and carry it up to the next level. *Pick up the ball of old yarn from below, bring it from under the new yarn to the front, wrap over the new yarn, then ch 1 with the new yarn*. Repeat from * to * for all but the last chain. Now you can drop the old yarn, turn, and work across with the new yarn.*

Once you've turned the work, rearrange the feeds so that the ball of old yarn you just dropped is positioned to the hook side. The working yarn ball and ball of next yarn hanging off the far end of the row should now be at the nonhook side.

Remember to change yarns every row. This seems like a lot of work and fuss, but examine the row edges after a few rows and you'll appreciate how neatly the strands are contained and how cool it looks. Really. Sort of barber-pole-ish. I think it's almost a shame to cover up those wraps with finishing stitches.

Instructions

With MC1, fsc 145 to measure approximately 48" (122cm). Turn the foundation over so sc edge is on top, then begin to work across the sc edge.

HEADER (RS): Continuing with MC1, ch 4, hdc in the first sc; [skip the next 2 sc, (hdc, ch 2, hdc) in the next sc] 47 times; skip the next 2 sc, (hdc, ch 4, sl st) in the last sc; do not turn.

Rotate the foundation so the chain edge is on top, and begin to work across the chain edge.

ROW 1 (RS): Continuing with MC1, ch 5, Eshell in the first ch; skip the next 3 chs, sc in the next ch; ch 3, sc in the next ch, skip the next 3 chs, [(Eshell, ch 3, Eshell) in the next ch, skip the next 3 chs, sc in the next ch; ch 3, sc in the next ch, skip the next 3 chs] 15 times; (Eshell, ch 1, tr) in the last ch, joining and changing to CC in the last tr; turn—31 ch-3 sps.

Create two angles, one on each side of the ch-3 sp at the center of the foundation (center back neck).

ROW 2 (WS): With CC, ch 4 *(equals dc, ch 1)*, sc in the beginning ch-sp, [(Eshell, ch 3, Eshell) in the next ch-3 sp, (sc, ch 3, sc) in the next ch-3 sp] 7 times; work a fan in the

next ch-3 sp, (sc, ch 3, sc) in the next ch-3 sp, work a fan in the next ch-3 sp, [(sc, ch 3, sc) in the next ch-3 sp; (Eshell, ch 3, Eshell) in the next ch-3 sp] 7 times; [sc, ch 1, dc] in the turning chain space, joining and changing to MC2 in the last dc; turn—35 ch-3 sps.

Mark the middle (second) ch-3 sp of each of the two fans at the center back; move or wrap the markers up as you go into the ch-3 sp at the center of the angle.

Maintain the ends of the rows in the Angular Momentum sequence; maintain the color sequence of one row each in three balls of yarn, carrying and wrapping the unused strands at each end, and changing to the next yarn every row; work a fan at the center back markers every third row.

ROW 3: With MC2, work Pattern Row B.

ROW 4: With MC1, work Pattern Row A.

ROW 5: With CC, begin as Pattern Row B, [work in pattern as established to the next marked ch-3 sp of the angle; work a fan in the marked ch-3 sp] 2 times, then complete the row in pattern as established, ending as Pattern Row B—39 ch-3 sps.

ROW 6: With MC2, work Pattern Row A.

ROW 7: With MC1, work Pattern Row B.

ROW 8: With CC, begin as Pattern Row A, [work in pattern as established to the next marked ch-3 sp of the angle; work a fan in the marked ch-3 sp] 2 times, then complete the row in pattern as established, ending as Pattern Row A—43 ch-3 sps.

ROWS 9–29: Repeat Rows 3–8 3 times, then repeat Rows 3–5—71 ch-3 sps.

End yarns MC1 and CC, continue with MC2.

The markers should still be in the second (middle) ch-3 sp at each of the two angles. Shift the markers to roughly the middle of the sides: moving toward the end of the row, skip the next 11 ch-3 sps from the center ch-3 sp of one angle, place the marker in the next ch-3 sp; do the same with the other marker. *Leave these markers in place; do not move them up.* This gives you an idea where the line of the shoulder will be and helps with cuff placement later.

ROW 30: With MC2, ch 3, sc in the beginning sp; [ch 3, sc in the next ch-3 sp, ch 3, (sc, ch 3, sc) in the next ch-3 sp] 35 times; ch 3, sc in the next ch-3 sp; ch 3, sc in the turning chain space; ch 3, sl st in the 4th ch of the turning chain; turn—109 ch-3 sps.

Finishing

With the right side now facing and continuing with MC2, work a finishing round of sc across all edges.

FINISHING RND (RS): Ch 1, 3 sc in each ch-3 sp across the last row. Rotate the work, then 3 sc in the next tr row edge, [2 sc in the next dc row edge, 3 sc in the next tr row edge] 14 times; sc in the foundation sc row edge; 4 sc in the beginning ch-4 sp of the header. Rotate the work, then 3 sc in each ch-2 sp across the header; 4 sc in the last ch-4 sp of the header. Rotate the work, then sc in the foundation sc row edge; 3 sc in the next tr row edge; [2 sc in the next dc row edge; 3 sc in the next tr row edge] 14 times; sl st in the beginning sc. Fasten off.

Weave in the ends, and block, leaving the markers in place.

Cuffs

Go to one of the shoulder line markers, located at roughly the center ch-3 sp of Row 29 at one side of the wrap. In that ch-3 sp there should now be a sc from making Row 30. In the row above that, there are sc stitches on either side from making the Finishing Rnd. Moving forward from the marker, skip 11 sc stitches of the Finishing Rnd forward, and mark the next sc; moving backward from the marker, skip 11 sc stitches of the Finishing Rnd back, and mark the next sc. Do the same on the other side of the wrap.

This portions out cuffs of 24 stitches that will measure approximately 8" (20.5cm) in circumference. For larger or smaller cuffs, add or omit sc to this count.

With the wrong side of one side facing, join either MC yarn with a sl st in the first marked sc.

RND 1 (WS): Ch 2 *(this equals hdc)*, skip the marked sc, hdc in each of the next 23 stitches, ending in the next marked sc; curve the section around so the edges meet; sl st in the 2nd ch of the beginning ch; turn—24 hdc.

RND 2 (RS): Ch 2, hdc through the front loop only in each of the next 23 hdc; sl st in the 2nd ch of the beginning ch; turn.

RNDS 3–10: Repeat Rnd 2 8 times or for the desired cuff length; do not turn.

The next finishing round of sc will give the cuff edge a little more stability and better wear.

RND 11: With the right side still facing, ch 1, sc in the first hdc, sc in each of the next 23 hdc; sl st in the beginning sc. Fasten off.

Make the cuff from marker to marker on other Sleeve in the same way. Weave in the ends.

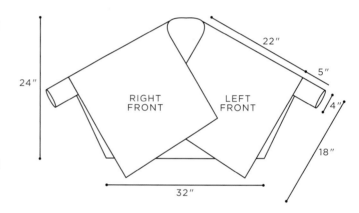

string theory

Entropy the doily has generated all the lace crochet elements that combine and recombine to make the designs in this book. In the three designs of String Theory, everything comes into play with strings attached.

The Galaxy Skirt (page 71) hinted that extra motifs could be added to an assembly. The design sets Kerry and Andromeda showcase what can be done by adding, omitting, and altering courses of motifs. The two sets of necklines, waist shapings, even the sleeves and lengths may be interchanged.

kerry

TOP AND SKIRT

kerry TOP AND SKIRT

Kerry begins innocently enough as a cap-shouldered top with a wide, rounded neck and header for stringing, to create an optional peasant-style neckline. The waist is deeply sculpted and flares to motif points that circle at high hip length and spill over the top of the matching skirt.

Worn upside down, Kerry's motif points drape with careless abandon around the neck and shoulders for a low, loose cowl, and the header sits at the waist to be cinched with a drawstring, or not. Stringing the top and skirt headers together turns Kerry into a breathtaking two-piece dress. It's a 1960s retro silhouette with a blouson waist, then sleek and slender through the hip.

skill level
EXPERIENCED ● ● ●

Size

Kerry Top
XS (S/M, L); sample shown is size S/M

Finished bust 36 (40, 44)" (91 [101.5, 112]cm); waist 26 (28, 32)" (66 [71, 81]cm); length 17½ (20, 21¾)" (44.5 [51, 55]cm)

For suggestions about extended sizing, see the Pattern Notes.

Kerry Skirt
XS (S/M, L); sample shown is size S/M

Finished waist 27 (27, 30)" (68.5 [68.5, 76]cm); full hip 36 (39, 42)" (91 [99, 106.5]cm); length 17½ (20, 21¾)" (44.5 [51, 55]cm)

Materials
Tahki Cotton Classic Lite, 100% mercerized cotton, 1¾ oz (50g), 146 yd (135m) Fine

For Top: 4 (4, 5) hanks in #4718 Celadon

For Skirt: 4 (5, 6) hanks in #4718 Celadon

U.S. Size G-6 (4mm) crochet hook for sizes XS (S/M), or size needed to obtain gauge

U.S. Size 7 (4.5mm) crochet hook for size L only, or size needed to obtain gauge

Stitch markers

Gauge (as crocheted)
For sizes XS (S/M): 18 fdc or sc = 4" (10cm)

For size L: 16 fdc or sc = 4" (10cm)

For Size XS

Carina Minor Pent Motif
RND 1: 1½" (3.8cm)

RND 2: 2¾" (7cm)

RND 5: one side, point to point = 4" (10cm); height = 5½" (14cm); widest point = 6" (15cm)

Carina Minor Hex Motif
RND 1: 2" (5cm)

RND 2: 3½" (9cm)

RND 5: one side, point to point = 4" (10cm); height = 6" (15cm); widest point = 7" (18cm)

For Size S/M

Carina Major Pent Motif
RND 1: 1½" (3.8cm)

RND 2: 2¾" (7cm)

RND 6: one side, point to point = 4½" (11.5cm); height = 6½" (16.5cm); widest point = 7" (18cm)

Carina Major Hex Motif
RND 1: 2" (5cm)

RND 2: 3½" (9cm)

RND 6: one side, point to point = 4½" (11.5cm); height = 6½" (16.5cm); widest point = 8" (20.5cm)

For Size L

Larger-Gauge Carina Major Pent Motif
RND 1: 1¾" (4.5cm)

RND 2: 3" (7.5cm)

RND 6: one side, point to point = 5" (12.5cm); height = 7" (18cm); widest point = 7½" (19cm)

Larger-Gauge Carina Major Hex Motif
RND 1: 2¼" (5.5cm)

RND 2: 3¾" (9.5cm)

RND 6: one side, point to point = 5" (12.5cm); height = 7" (18cm); widest point = 8½" (21.5cm)

Please see Measuring Motifs (page 35).

Stitch Definitions
See instructions for individual Carina motifs (page 25).

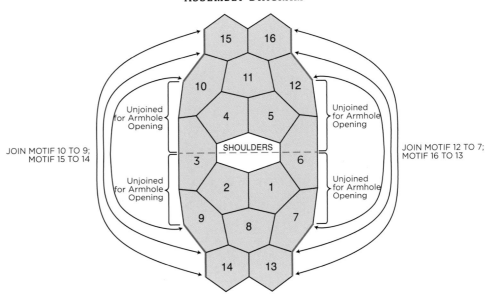

For skirt assembly diagram, see Galaxy Skirt (page 72).

For more motif assembly information, see Universal Assembly (page 33).

Pattern Notes

If you are willing to sacrifice the upside down-ability of this top, you can engineer a version that has a relaxed fit and six motifs instead of four around the waist, following the tips below for Straight Side Option. A major advantage to doing this is that you now have the option of adding to the length; crochet another course of six hex motifs for a tunic, two or three (or as many as you like) more courses for a dress length. This also makes it possible to extend the sizing by crocheting to a looser gauge. Choose a slightly thicker yarn and appropriate hook to make larger motifs.

For a drawstring waist skirt in extended sizing, add motifs to each course in the same way as Galaxy Skirt sizing (page 73) and apply a header instead of the elastic ribbing. Be advised that your headers will no longer match for stringing the top and skirt together for a dress.

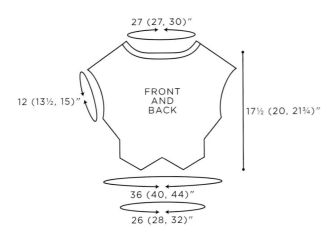

Kerry Top Instructions

Size XS uses the smaller hook and Carina minor motifs.

Size S/M uses the smaller hook and Carina major motifs.

Size L uses the larger hook and larger-gauge Carina major motifs.

Make and assemble 16 motifs, connecting each motif as you go while crocheting the last round according to assembly diagram.

All Sizes Upper Course (neckline and shoulders)

MOTIFS 1–6 (FOUR PENTS AND TWO HEXES): Connect into a ring, with one flat side of each motif at the neckline, and one hex at each shoulder.

Middle Course

MOTIFS 7–9 (HEXES): Connect completely to the Upper Course and to one another. Turn the body over.

MOTIF 10 (HEX): Connect completely to Motif 9 at the side of the body. Work the next 2 (3, 3) side ch-sps unattached for the armhole opening. Join the next point sp to the next free point sp of Motif 3, then connect the next side and point sp completely to the next side of Motif 3. Connect the next side completely to the next side of Motif 4, and then finish the rest of the motif.

MOTIF 11 (HEX): Connect completely at the center of the body to Motif 10, Motif 4, and Motif 5, then finish the rest of the motif.

MOTIF 12 (HEX): Connect completely to Motif 11, Motif 5, and Motif 6. Work the next 2 (3, 3) side ch-sps unattached for the armhole opening. Join the next point sp to the next free point sp of Motif 7. Connect the next side and point completely to Motif 7 at the side of the body, then finish the rest of the motif.

Lower Course

MOTIF 13: Join the first point sp to the lower join between Motifs 7 and 12, then connect completely to Motifs 7 and 8; finish the rest of the motif.

MOTIF 14: Connect completely to Motifs 13, 8, and 9, then finish the rest of the motif.

MOTIF 15: Join the first point sp to the next free point sp of Motif 14, then connect the next 2 (3, 3) side ch-sps to Motif 14. Join the next point sp in the triple join of Motifs 14, 9, and 10, and then connect completely to Motifs 10 and 11. Finish the rest of the motif.

MOTIF 16: Join the first point sp to the next free point sp of Motif 15, then connect completely to Motifs 15 and 11. Connect the next 2 (3, 3) side ch-sps to Motif 12. Join the next point sp in the triple join of Motifs 12, 7, and 13. Connect completely to Motif 13 and then finish the rest of the motif.

Neck Finishing

The Kerry top has a bound neckline with a header.

Fdc 120 to measure approximately 27 (27, 30)" (68.5 [68.5, 76]cm). *(To measure, stretch the foundation, let it snap back if it wants to, then measure end to end.)* Bring the ends of the foundation together, being careful not to twist the stitches. Sl st in the beginning dc (the 4th ch of the beginning ch 4) to form a ring. Begin to work across the dc edge of the foundation.

With the right side of the body facing, hold the foundation ring to the left (nonhook side) and the motif neck edge to the right (hook side). Bouncing back and forth, as you would to connect motif sides, connect the foundation to the 6 motif sides at the neck edge, using 20 foundation stitches per motif side. Size XS uses a relaxed connecting round; sizes S/M (L) use a controlled connecting round.

TIP: *Just before closing the following Connecting Rnd, bring the feeder yarn to the wrong side of the work so it is in the proper place to continue the header.*

Size XS Only

Begin with the first connection in the ch-4 side sp just past the sc at the center of a shoulder hex motif.

CONNECTING RND (RS): Ch 1, sc in the first dc of the foundation, *ch 2, sl st in the next ch-4 sp of the motif; ch 2, skip the next 3 dc of the foundation, sc in the next dc; ch 2, skip the next (sc, dc) of the motif, sl st in the next dc; ch 2, skip the next 3 dc of the foundation, sc in the next dc; ch 2, sl st in the next sl st. Join between the motifs, ch 2, skip the next 3 dc of the foundation, sc in the next dc; ch 2, skip the next 2 dc of the motif, sl st in the next dc; ch 2, skip the next 3 dc of the foundation, sc in the next dc; ch 2, sl st in the next ch-4 sp of the motif; ch 2, skip next 3 dc of the foundation, sc in the next dc*; repeat from * to * 5 times; on the final repeat, omit the last sc; instead, sl st in the beginning sc. Continue with the header—30 ch-sp joins.

Sizes S/M (L/XL)

Begin with the first connection in the ch-4 side sp at the center of a shoulder hex motif.

CONNECTING RND (RS): Ch 1, sc in the first stitch of the double crochet foundation, *[ch 2, sl st in next ch-4 sp of the motif, ch 2, skip the next 3 dc of the foundation, sc in the next dc] 2 times; ch 2, sl st in the next partial ch-sp before the motif join; ch 2, skip the next 3 dc of the foundation, sc in the next dc; ch 2, sl st in the next partial ch-sp of the past motif join; ch 2, skip the next 3 dc of the foundation, sc in the next dc; ch 2, sl st in the next ch-4 sp of the motif; ch 2, skip the next 3 dc of the foundation, sc in the next dc*; repeat from * to * 5 times; on the final repeat, omit the last sc; instead, sl st in the beginning sc. Continue with the header—30 (30) ch-sp joins.

Header

Rotate the piece so the chain edge of the foundation is on top (the feeder yarn is now to the wrong side, inside of the body). Sl st in the stem of the beginning sc of the Connecting Rnd (the one just joined in), then sl st in each of the next 3 chains of the beginning end of the foundation just above. Reach across the

gap and sl st in the last ch of the foundation, then begin to work around the chain edge.

HEADER RND 1 (RS): Ch 4 *(this equals hdc, ch 2)*, hdc in same foundation ch; [skip next 2 chains, (hdc, ch 2, hdc) in the next ch] 39 times; skip the last 2 ch sts, sl st in the 2nd ch of the beginning ch—40 ch-2 sps.

HEADER RND 2 (RS): Ch 1, 3 sc in each ch-2 sp around; sl st in the beginning sc, and fasten off—120 sc.

Weave in the ends, and block.

If desired, make a neck drawstring (page 137).

For Straight Side Option

Change the assembly of the Middle Course of motifs for a top without waist shaping. For the same Kerry top length, add the Lower Course requiring 6 hex motifs. This straight assembly allows the top to be lengthened by adding motif courses.

UPPER COURSE: Connect Motifs 1–6 in same way.

MIDDLE COURSE: Connect hex Motifs 7–12 to the Upper Course in same way as Andromeda Second Course hex Motifs 7–12 (page 127).

LOWER COURSE (6 HEXES): Make hex Motifs 13–18, connecting completely in a ring to the motifs of the Middle Course and to one another.

Add courses of 6 hexes as desired to lengthen. Finish with the neck header in the same way.

Kerry Skirt Instructions

Size XS uses the smaller hook and Carina minor motifs.

Size S/M uses the smaller hook and Carina major motifs.

Size L uses the larger hook and Carina major motifs.

Make and assemble 18 motifs, connecting each motif as you go while crocheting the last round according to the assembly diagram for Galaxy Skirt size XS/S (page 72).

FIT TIP: *Kerry Skirt may be shortened to micro-mini length by omitting the Lower Course of six hexes, or lengthened by adding courses of hexes as desired.*

Waist Finishing

Fdc 120 (120, 120). Connect to the motif waist edge and add a header in same way as the Kerry neck finishing according to your size (page 124). Weave in the ends, and block.

String

The skirt requires a drawstring. Choose a string type (page 137) as desired, and make one string 45 (45, 50)" (114 [114, 127]cm) long or to taste. Weave the string in and out of the spaces between the hdc Vs of the header.

To make a two-piece dress, with the right sides facing, slip the header of the skirt over the header of the top. Matching the holes, weave the string in and out through both thicknesses, with the ends centered at the front.

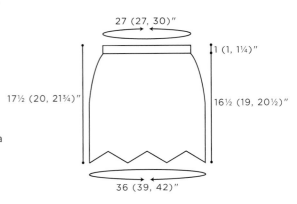

andromeda

Andromeda is a double V-neck top construction that has endless possibilities.

andromeda VEST

Sleeveless and cropped, with a narrow foundation binding at neck, armholes, and waist, the vest version distills the key elements of the Andromeda motif construction down to their simplest form. Crocheted in a soft, stretchy sock yarn, the vest fabric has plenty of give to fit a range of sizes.

skill level

INTERMEDIATE ● ● ○

Size

S (M/L, XL); sample shown is size S

Finished bust 38 (42½, 47)" (96.5 [108, 119]cm); waist: 26½ (32, 36)" (67 [81, 91]cm); length 17½ (19½, 21)" (44.5 [49.5, 53.5]cm)

Materials

Kollage Sock-a-licious, 70% superwash merino wool, 10% mulberry silk, 20% nylon, 3½ oz (100g), 354 yd (324m) **2** Fine

2 (3, 3) hanks in #7807 Heather

U.S. Size G-6 (4mm) crochet hook for sizes S (M/L), or size needed to obtain gauge

U.S. Size G-7 (4.5mm) crochet hook for size XL, or size needed to obtain gauge

Stitch markers

Gauge

FOR SIZES S (M/L): 18 fsc or sc = 4" (10cm)

FOR SIZE XL: 16 fsc or sc = 4" (10cm)

For Size S

Copernicus Minor Square Motif

RND 2: 1¾" (4.5cm)

RND 3: 3½" (9cm)

RND 5: one side = 4¼" (11cm); widest point = 6" (15cm)

Copernicus Minor Pent Motif

RND 3: 2⅜" (6cm)

RND 4: 4" (10cm)

RND 6: one side, point to point = 4" (10cm); height = 5½" (14cm); widest point = 6" (15cm)

Copernicus Minor Hex Motif

RND 3: 2¾" (7cm)

RND 4: 4½" (11.5cm)

RND 6: one side, point to point = 4" (10cm); height = 6" (15cm); widest point = 7" (18cm)

For Size M/L

Copernicus Major Square Motif

RND 2: 1¾" (4.5cm)

RND 3: 3½" (9cm)

RND 6: one side, point to point = 4¾" (12cm); widest point = 6½" (16.5cm)

Copernicus Major Pent Motif

RND 3: 2⅜" (6cm)

RND 4: 4" (10cm)

RND 7: one side, point to point = 4½" (11.5cm); height = 6¼" (16cm); widest point = 7" (18cm)

Copernicus Major Hex Motif

RND 3: 2¾" (7cm)

RND 4: 4½" (11.5cm)

RND 7: one side, point to point = 4½" (11.5cm); height = 6½" (16.5cm); widest point = 7¾" (20cm)

For Size XL

Larger-Gauge Copernicus Major Square Motif

RND 2: 2⅛" (5.3cm)

RND 3: 3⅞" (9.7cm)

RND 6: one side = 5" (12.5cm); widest point = 7" (18cm)

Larger-Gauge Copernicus Major Pent Motif

RND 3: 2⅝" (6.7cm)

RND 4: 4½" (11.5cm)

RND 7: one side, point to point = 5" (12.5cm); height = 7" (18cm); widest point = 7½" (19cm)

Larger-Gauge Copernicus Major Hex Motif

RND 3: 3" (7.5cm)

RND 4: 5" (12.5cm)

RND 7: one side, point to point = 5" (12.5cm); height = 7¼" (18.5cm); widest point = 8½" (21.5cm)

Please see Measuring Motifs (page 35).

Stitch Definitions

FSC (FOUNDATION SINGLE CROCHET): See Chainless Foundations (page 140)

See stitches and instructions for individual Copernicus motifs (page 22).

For more motif assembly information, see Universal Assembly (page 33).

Instructions

Size S uses the smaller hook and Copernicus minor motifs.

Size M/L uses the smaller hook and Copernicus major motifs.

Size XL uses the larger hook and larger-gauge Copernicus major motifs.

Assemble 18 Copernicus motifs (4 squares, 8 hexes, 6 pents), connecting each motif as you go while crocheting the last round according to the assembly diagram (see Andromeda Dress assembly diagram, page 132).

First Course (neckline and shoulders)

MOTIFS 1–6 (4 SQUARES AND 2 HEXES): Connect into a ring, with one flat side of each motif at the neckline, and one hex at each shoulder. Square 1 is connected to Square 2 at one point sp only; Square 4 is connected to Square 5 at one point sp only. These are the points of the front and back V-neck.

Second Course

MOTIFS 7–9 (HEXES): Connect completely to the First Course and to one another; turn the body over.

MOTIF 10 (HEX): Join the first point sp to the next free point sp of Motif 9 at the underarm. Work the next 2 (3, 3) side ch-sps unattached (for the armhole opening), then join the next point sp to the next free point sp of Motif 3. Connect completely to Motif 3 and Motif 4, and finish the rest of the motif.

MOTIF 11 (HEX): Connect completely at the center of the body to Motif 10, Motif 4, and Motif 5, then finish the rest of the motif.

MOTIF 12 (HEX): Connect completely to Motif 11, Motif 5, and Motif 6. Work the next 2 (3, 3) side ch-sps unattached (for the armhole opening), then join the next point sp to the next free point sp of Motif 7 at the underarm. Finish the rest of the motif.

Third Course

MOTIFS 13–18 (6 PENTS): Connect completely in a ring to the motifs of the Second Course and to one another.

Finishing

The neck, armholes, and bottom edges are all finished with a relaxed edging, using 20 (24, 24) stitches of the foundation for each motif, except at the notch of the front and back V-neck, where there is a little shaping.

Neckline

All sizes use the smaller G-6 (4 mm) hook.

Mark the join between square motifs 1 and 2, and between squares 4 and 5 for the V-neck points. Attenuate the V-neck shaping by allowing 2 fewer foundation stitches at each neck point.

Fsc 116 (140, 140) to measure approximately 26 (31, 31)" (66 [79, 79]cm). (To measure, stretch the foundation, let it snap back if it wants to, and measure end to end.) Bring the ends of the foundation together, being careful not to twist the stitches; sl st in the beginning sc to form a ring, and begin to work around the sc edge.

With the right sides of the motifs facing, hold the foundation ring to the nonhook side and the motif neck edge to the hook side. Bouncing back and forth, as you would to connect the motif sides, connect the foundation to the 6 motif sides at the neck edge, using 20 (24, 24) foundation stitches per motif side except at the V notch at the front and back.

TIP: *If continuing with a header as in the Andromeda Dress (page 131), before closing any of the connecting rounds, bring the feeder yarn to the wrong side of the work so it is in the proper place.*

Locate the hex motif at one shoulder; for size S, begin connecting in the ch-4 sp past the sc at the center of the motif side; for size M/L (XL), begin connecting in the next ch-4 sp past the ch-4 sp at the center of the motif.

NECK CONNECTING RND WITH V SHAPING

(RS): Ch 1, sc in the first sc of the foundation; *ch 2, sl st in the next ch-4 sp of the motif; ch 2, skip the next 3 sc of the foundation; sc in the next sc; ch 2, skip the next (sc and dc) of the motif, and sl st in the next dc; ch 2, skip the next 3 sc of the foundation, sc in the next sc**; ch 2, sl st in the next sl st join between the motifs; ch 2, skip the next 3 sc of the foundation; sc in the next sc; ***ch 2, skip the next 2 dc of the motif; sl st in the next dc; ch 2, skip the next 3 sc of the foundation, sc in the next sc; [ch 2, sl st in the next ch-4 sp of the motif; ch 2, skip the next 3 sc of the foundation; sc in the next sc] 1 (2, 2) times*; repeat from * to **. For V shaping, ch 1, sl st in the next marked sl st join between the squares; ch 1, skip the next sc of the foundation; sc in the next sc. Repeat from *** to *; repeat from * to * 2 times across 2 motif sides, then repeat from * to **; for V shaping, ch 1, sl st in the next marked sl st join between squares; ch 1, skip the next sc of the foundation, sc in the next sc. Repeat from *** to *, then repeat from * to * across the last motif side; on the final repeat, omit the last sc; instead, sl st in beginning sc. Fasten off.

Armholes

For S (M/L) use G-6 hook; for XL use G-7.

Fsc 60 (72, 72) to measure approximately 13½ (16, 18)" (34.5 [40.5, 45.5]cm). Bring the ends of the foundation together, being careful not to twist the stitches, and sl st in the beginning sc to form a ring, then begin to work around the sc edge. With the right sides of the motifs of one armhole facing, begin connecting in the join among the 3 motifs at the underarm.

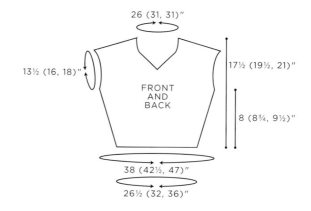

26 (31, 31)"

13½ (16, 18)"

FRONT AND BACK

17½ (19½, 21)"

8 (8¾, 9½)"

38 (42½, 47)"

26½ (32, 36)"

ARMHOLE CONNECTING RND (RS): Ch 1, sc in the first sc of the foundation; *ch 2, sl st in the next sl st join between the motifs; ch 2, skip the next 3 sc of the foundation, sc in the next sc; ch 2, skip the next 2 dc of the motif, sl st in next dc; ch 2, skip the next 3 sc of the foundation, sc in the next sc; [ch 2, sl st in the next ch-4 sp of the motif; ch 2, skip the next 3 sc of the foundation; sc in the next sc] 2 (3, 3) times; ch 2, skip the next (sc and dc of the motif), sl st in the next dc; ch 2, skip the next 3 sc of the foundation; sc in the next sc*; repeat from * to * 2 times across the 2 remaining motif sides; on the final repeat, omit the last sc; instead, sl st in the beginning sc. Fasten off.

Finish the other armhole edge in the same way.

Waist

The unbound sides of the pents at the waist edge tend to stretch out. Binding the lower edge will help stabilize the waist.

For S (M/L), use G-6 hook; for XL, use G-7.

Fsc 120 (144, 144) to measure approximately 26½ (32, 36)" (67 [81, 91]cm). Bring the ends of the foundation together, being careful not to twist the stitches, and sl st in the beginning sc to form a ring; then begin to work around the single crochet edge. With the right sides of the motifs of the waist facing, begin connecting in the join between the motifs at one side of the body.

WAIST CONNECTING RND (RS): Make in same way as the Armhole Connecting Rnd, working across 6 motif sides.

Weave in the ends, and block.

andromeda PEPLUM VEST

The addition of a header to the waist of the Andromeda Vest opens up the option of stringing on other stuff. You could attach an entire skirt in the same way that the Kerry Top and Skirt go together. Or, as shown, you can convert the vest into a short-skirted tunic. This pretty little ruffled peplum may look familiar. It is essentially a mini version of the T-Bird Stole (page 106), except with a more gathered top edge.

skill level
INTERMEDIATE ● ● ○

Size

To coordinate with Vest sizes S (M/L, XL); sample shown is size S

Finished waist 26½ (32, 36)"; length 9 (9, 10)"

Materials

Elsebeth Lavold Hempathy, 34% hemp, 41% cotton, 25% modal; 1¾ oz (50g), 154 yd (141m) **2** Fine

6 (7, 8) balls for Peplum Vest as shown

OR approximately 250–300 yd sock/fingering weight yarn for Peplum only

U.S. Size G-6 (4mm) crochet hook for sizes S (M/L)

U.S. Size 7 (4.5mm) crochet hook for size XL

Gauge

For sizes S (M/L): 18 fsc or sc = 4" (10cm); in Angular Momentum stitch pattern, one repeat = 2¼"; 4 rows = 2¼"

For size XL: 16 fsc or sc = 4" (10cm); in Angular Momentum stitch pattern, one repeat = 2½"; 4 rows = 2½"

Stitch Definitions

FSC (FOUNDATION SINGLE CROCHET): See Chainless Foundations (page 140).

See Angular Momentum Stitch Pattern (page 98) for stitches and pattern rows.

See Corsair Collar (page 102) for Corsair pattern rows.

Instructions

Make the Andromeda Vest (page 126); after Waist Connecting Rnd, do not fasten off. Continue to make a header in the same way as Andromeda Dress Sleeve Header (page 134) for 40 (48, 48) ch-2 sps; fasten off.

Peplum

With same hook size as used for vest, fsc 121 (145, 145) to measure approximately 26½ (32, 36)"; turn the foundation over so the sc edge is on top, begin working across the sc edge. Make the header first.

HEADER (RS): Ch 4, hdc in the first sc, skip the next 2 sc, [(hdc, ch 2, hdc) in the next sc, skip the next 2 sc] 39 (47, 47) times; (hdc, ch 4, sl st) in the last sc; do not turn—41 (49, 49) ch-sps.

Rotate the foundation so the chain edge is on top; begin working across the chain edge.

ROW 1: Ch 5, Eshell in the first ch, skip the next 3 chs, (sc, ch 3, sc) in the next ch, [skip the next 3 chs, (Eshell, ch 3, Eshell) in the next ch, skip the next 3 chs, (sc, ch 3, sc) in the next ch] 14 (17, 17) times; skip the next 3 chs, (Eshell, ch 1, tr) in the last ch; turn—14 (17, 17) points plus half points at the ends.

ROWS 2–5: Work the Angular Momentum Stitch Pattern [Pattern Row A, Pattern Row B] (page 98) 2 times.

ROW 6: Ch 4, dc in the beginning sp, *ch 2, dc in each of next 3 dc, ch 2, skip the next ch-3 sp *(between sc)*, dc in each of the next 3 dc, ch 2**, (dc, ch 3, dc) in the next ch-3 sp *(between Eshells)**; repeat from * to * 13 (16, 16) times, the repeat from * to **, end with (dc, ch 1, dc) in the tch sp, turn—4 (17, 17) Corsair points plus half points at ends.

ROWS 7–12: Work in same way as Corsair Collar Rows 4–9 (page 102).

Rotate the piece and continue to work a finishing row of sc across the row edges of the two short sides and across the header.

FINISHING ROW (RS): [2 sc in the next dc row edge, 3 sc in the next tr row edge] 5 times, sc in fsc row edge, 4 sc in the beginning ch-4 sp of the header, 3 sc in each ch-2 sp of header, 4 sc in the last ch-4 sp of the header; sc in fsc row edge, [3 sc in the next tr row edge, 2 sc in the next dc row edge] 5 times, 4 dc in the last tr row edge, ch 4, sl st in 3rd ch of beginning ch. Fasten off.

Weave ends, block peplum.

String

Make a drawstring for the waist as desired (page 137). With the right sides facing, match the header holes of the Peplum with those of the waist edge of Vest, with the Peplum opening to one side of body as shown or as desired. Weave string in and out of holes through both thicknesses, tie ends. You may also make buttons (page 138) as desired to close the Peplum edges (not shown).

andromeda DRESS

With the addition of elbow-length sleeves and a short, slim skirt, Andromeda becomes a shapely little dress. For a sweet touch, make the separate Add-on Flutter Sleeves (page 135) to string whenever you please.

skill level
EXPERIENCED ● ● ●

Size

XS/S (M, L); sample shown is size XS/S

Finished bust 36 (40½, 45)" (91 [103, 114]cm); waist 25½ (27, 30)" (65 [68.5, 76]cm); full hip 36 (39, 43½)" (91 [99, 110]cm); length 33 (37, 40½)" (84 [94, 103]cm)

Materials

Elsebeth Lavold Hempathy, 34% hemp, 41% cotton, 25% modal, 1¾ oz (50g), 153 yd (140m) Fine

9 (11, 13) balls in #4 White Beach for dress and pair of Flutter Sleeves

U.S. Size G-6 (4mm) crochet hook for sizes XS/S (M) and for all sizes finishing, or size needed to obtain gauge

U.S. Size 7 (4.5mm) crochet hook for size L or size needed to obtain gauge

Stitch markers

Gauge

Same as Andromeda Vest (page 126) for fsc, sc, and motifs

Stitch Definitions

FSC (FOUNDATION SINGLE CROCHET): See Chainless Foundations (page 140).

See stitches and instructions for individual Copernicus motifs (page 22).

For more motif assembly information, see Universal Assembly (page 33).

Pattern Notes

The sizing of this dress is different and more limited than for Andromeda Vest because of the addition of sleeves and a skirt. The bust is roomy, but the waist and hip are slim-fitting. The weight of the skirt tends to draw down the waist shaping, making it even slimmer and lower on the body. The armhole seems really small, but it hits farther down the upper arm because the shoulder is capped and the underarm is dropped. There is plenty of stretch in the fabric to fit most average figures, but if worked any larger using this assembly, the dress has increasingly nonhuman proportions.

If the waist shaping is too small, or if the shaping will land in the wrong place if you are short or short-waisted, you may easily adjust the dress for a straight-sided fit, equal to the full hip circumference through the waist. Instead of making pents for the Third Course (Motifs 13-18) and Fourth Course (Motifs 19-24), make and assemble 12 hexes. This will rotate the relative positions of the motif points of the Fifth and Sixth Courses with no harm done. This will ease the waist problem and should not significantly alter the length, but it will require more yarn. This also makes it possible to extend the sizing by crocheting to a looser gauge. Choose a slightly thicker yarn and appropriate hook to make larger motifs.

ASSEMBLY DIAGRAM

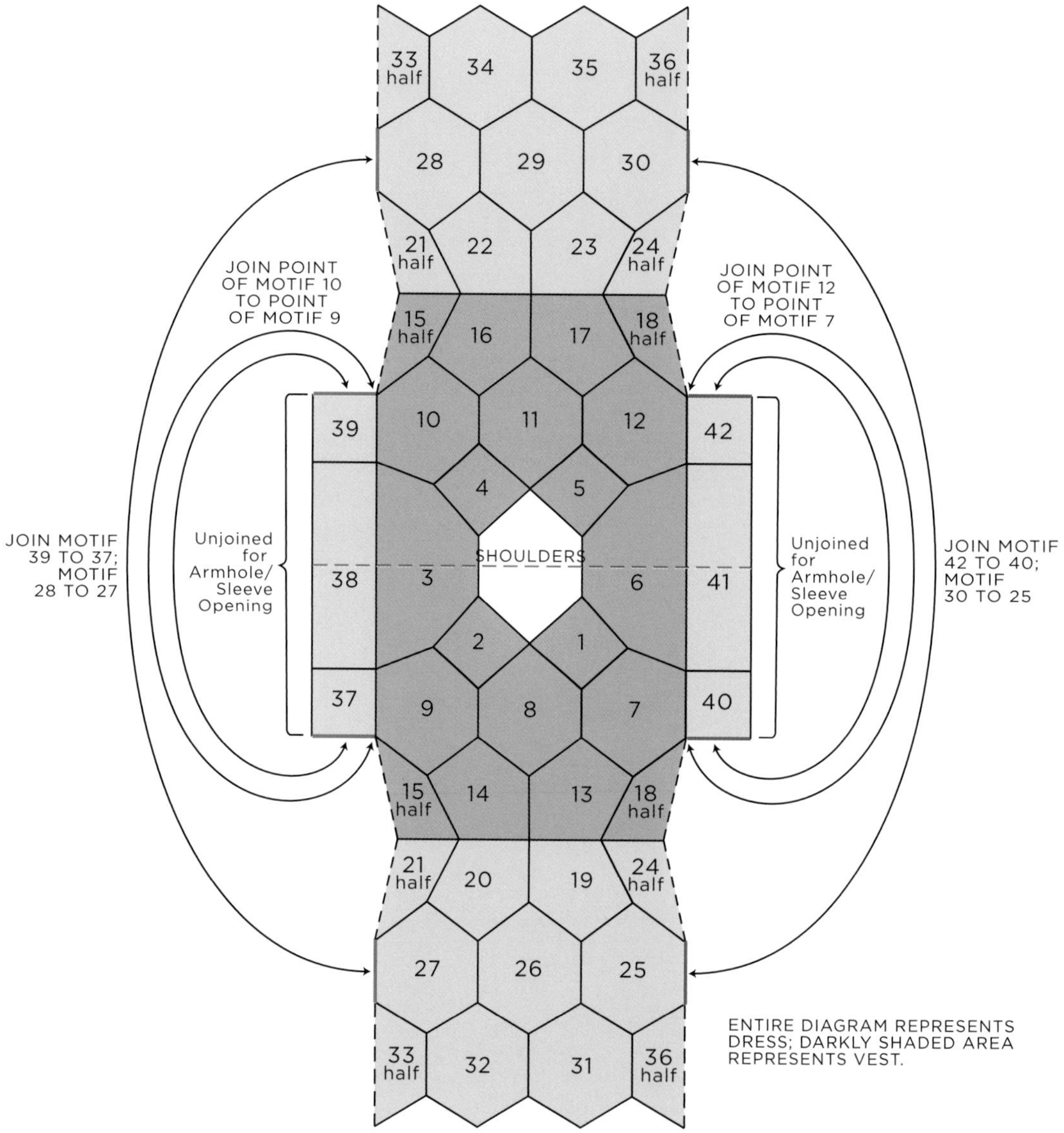

JOIN POINT OF MOTIF 10 TO POINT OF MOTIF 9

JOIN POINT OF MOTIF 12 TO POINT OF MOTIF 7

JOIN MOTIF 39 TO 37; MOTIF 28 TO 27

JOIN MOTIF 42 TO 40; MOTIF 30 TO 25

Unjoined for Armhole/Sleeve Opening

Unjoined for Armhole/Sleeve Opening

SHOULDERS

ENTIRE DIAGRAM REPRESENTS DRESS; DARKLY SHADED AREA REPRESENTS VEST.

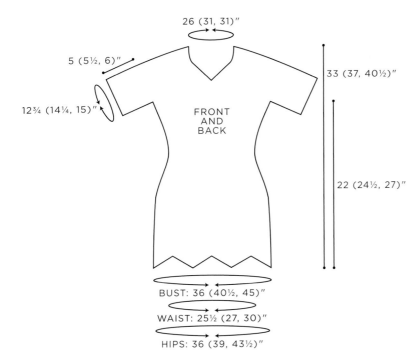

26 (31, 31)"

5 (5½, 6)"

12¾ (14¼, 15)"

33 (37, 40½)"

FRONT
AND
BACK

22 (24½, 27)"

BUST: 36 (40½, 45)"

WAIST: 25½ (27, 30)"

HIPS: 36 (39, 43½)"

Instructions

Size XS/S uses the smaller hook and Copernicus minor motifs.

Size M uses the smaller hook and Copernicus major motifs.

Size L uses the larger hook and larger-gauge Copernicus major motifs.

The dress is constructed of 42 motifs (10 squares, 12 pents, 20 hexes).

Top

The top part of the dress is assembled in same way as the sleeveless Andromeda Vest (page 127) First, Second, and Third Courses.

MOTIFS 1–18: Make in same way as Andromeda Sleeveless Vest Motifs 1–18 (page 127).

Skirt
Fourth Course

MOTIFS 19–24 (PENTS): Connect six pents completely in a ring to the motifs of the Third Course and to one another.

Fifth Course

MOTIFS 25–30 (HEXES): Connect six hexes completely in a ring to the motifs of the Fourth Course and to one another.

Sixth Course

MOTIFS 31–36 (HEXES): Connect six hexes completely in a ring to the motifs of the Fifth Course and to one another.

Sleeves

Sleeves are tubes of 3 squares each, attached to the three motif sides at the armhole edges.

First Sleeve

MOTIFS 37–39 (SQUARES): Connect three squares completely in a ring to the armhole edges of Motifs 9, 3, and 10, and to one another.

Second Sleeve

MOTIFS 40–42 (SQUARES): Connect three squares completely in a ring to the armhole edges of Motifs 7, 6, and 12, and to one another.

Finishing
Neckline

The dress neckline is finished with a foundation connected to the motif neck edge in same way as the Andromeda Vest, with an added header.

All sizes use the smaller hook.

Fsc 116 (140, 140), and join into a ring in same way as for Andromeda Vest Neckline (page 127).

NECK CONNECTING RND (RS): Make the Neck Connecting Rnd in the same way as for Andromeda Vest (page 126). Do not fasten off, do not turn; continue with header.

Mark the notch of the V-neck by moving up each of the two markers from the join of the square motifs into the skipped foundation stitch above.

TIP: *Remember, just before closing the Neck Connecting Rnd, bring the feeder yarn to the wrong side of the work so it is in the proper place to continue the header.*

Rotate so the chain edge of the foundation is on top.

HEADER RND 1 (RS): With the feeder yarn now at the back of the work, sl st in the stem of same sc of the Connecting Rnd as last joined, then sl st in the foundation st just above (with the yarn tail coming out of it). *Size M (L) only:* Reach across the gap between the ends of the foundation and sl st in the next ch of the foundation. All sizes: Ch 4 *(this equals hdc, ch 2)*, and hdc in the same foundation st. Now working across the chain edge of the foundation, [skip next 2 chs, (hdc, ch 2, hdc) in the next ch] 9 (10, 10) times, to one ch before the V notch marker. *Skip the next 3 chains *(centered at the V notch)*, [hdc, ch 2, hdc] in the next ch*; [skip the next 2 chs, (hdc, ch 2, hdc) in the next ch] 18 (22, 22) times to one ch before the next V notch marker; repeat from * to *; [skip next 2 chs, (hdc, ch 2, hdc) in the next ch] 8 (11, 11) times; skip the last 2 chs, sl st in the 2nd ch of the beginning ch—38 (46, 46) ch-2 sps.

HEADER RND 2 (RS): Ch 1, 3 sc in each ch-2 sp around; sl st in the beginning sc. Fasten off.

Sleeves

The Sleeves are finished with a foundation connected to the motif edge plus an added header.

For sizes XS/S (M), use the smaller hook; for size L, use the larger hook.

Fsc 60 (60, 60) to measure approximately 13½ (13½, 15)" (34.5 [34.5, 38]cm). Bring the ends of the foundation together, being careful not to twist the stitches, then sl st in the beginning sc to form a ring. Begin to work around the sc edge.

SIZE XS/S

With the right side of the motifs of one Sleeve facing, begin connecting in the join between the 2 motifs at the underarm.

SLEEVE CONNECTING RND (RS): Make in same way as the Andromeda Vest Armhole Connecting Rnd (page 128); do not fasten off. Continue with the header.

SIZES M (L)

With the right side of the motifs of one Sleeve facing, begin connecting in the partial ch-sp past the join between the 2 motifs at the underarm.

SLEEVE CONNECTING RND (RS): Ch 1, sc in the first sc of the foundation; *ch 2, sl st in the next partial ch-sp past the motif join; ch 2, skip the next 3 sc of the foundation, sc in the next sc; [ch 2, sl st in the next ch-4 sp of the motif; ch 2, skip the next 3 sc of the foundation, sc in the next sc] 3 times; ch 2, sl st in the next partial ch-sp before the motif join; ch 2, skip the next 3 sc of the founda-

tion, then sc in the next sc *; repeat from * to * 2 times; on the final repeat, omit the last sc; instead, sl st in the beginning sc. Continue with the header.

ALL SIZES Sleeve Header

SLEEVE HEADER RND 1 (RS): Ch 4 *(this equals hdc, ch 2)*, hdc in same foundation ch; [skip the next 2 chs, (hdc, ch 2, hdc) in the next ch] 19 times; skip the last 2 chs; sl st in the 2nd ch of the beginning ch—20 ch-2 sps.

SLEEVE HEADER RND 2 (RS): Ch 1, 3 sc in each ch-2 sp around; sl st in the beginning sc. Fasten off—60 sc.

Finish the other Sleeve edge in the same way.

Weave in the ends, and block.

add-on FLUTTER SLEEVES

These optional sleeves coordinate with Andromeda Sleeve headers; they are meant to be strung, cinched, and gathered.

skill level

EASY

Size

Finished depth 7½" (19cm); circumference, header 13½" (34.5cm); circumference, bottom 30" (76cm)

Materials

See Andromeda Dress (page 131)

U.S. Size G-6 (4 mm) crochet hook or size needed to obtain gauge

Gauge

18 fsc or sc = 4" (10cm)

Stitch Definitions

FSC (FOUNDATION SINGLE CROCHET): See Chainless Foundations (page 140).

See Entropy (page 11) for Corsair stitches, stitch pattern rounds, and stitch diagram.

Instructions

These ruffled cuffs are Corsair stitch pattern rounds crocheted onto a header ring, worked with the right side always facing.

Fsc 60 to measure approximately 13½" (34.5cm). Bring the ends of the foundation together, being careful not to twist the stiches, then sl st in the beginning sc to form a ring. Begin to work around the sc edge.

HEADER RND 1 (RS): Ch 4 *(this equals hdc, ch 2)*, hdc in same sc; [skip the next 2 sc, (hdc, ch 2, hdc) in the next sc] 19 times; skip the last 2 sc, sl st in the 2nd ch of the beginning ch—20 ch-2 sps.

HEADER RND 2 (RS): Ch 1, 3 sc in each ch-2 sp around; sl st in the beginning sc—60 sc.

Rotate so the chain edge of the foundation is on top, then sl st in the stem of the same sc of the Header Rnd just joined. Sl st in each of the next 2 chs of the beginning ch of Header Rnd 1; sl st in the foundation st just above (with the yarn tail in it). Begin to work across the chain edge of the foundation.

RND 1: Ch 5 *(this equals dc, ch 2)*, skip the first ch; [skip the next 2 chs, sc in the next ch; ch 2, skip the next 2 chs, (dc, ch 3, dc) in the next ch; ch 2] 9 times; skip the next 2 chs, sc in the next ch; ch 2, skip the last 2 chs, dc in the beginning ch; ch 1, hdc in the 3rd ch of the beginning ch *(this equals ch 3)*—10 ch-3 sps.

RND 2: Ch 3, 2 dc in the beginning sp; ch 3, skip the next 2 ch-2 sps, [(3 dc, ch 4, 3 dc) in next ch-3 sp; ch 3, skip the next 2 ch-2 sps] 9 times; dc in the beginning sp; ch 1, dc in the 3rd ch of the beginning ch *(this equals ch 4)*—10 Corsair repeats.

RND 3: Ch 5 *(this equals dc, ch 2)*, *dc in each of the next 3 dc stitches; ch 2, dc in each of the next 3 dc; ch 2**, (dc, ch 3, dc) in the next ch-4 sp; ch 2*; repeat from * to * 8 times, then repeat from * to **; dc in the beginning sp; ch 1, hdc in the 3rd ch of the beginning ch *(this equals ch 3)*.

RNDS 4–7: Same as Rnds 19–22 of Entropy (page 14), *except* work only 10 Corsair stitch repeats.

RND 8: Ch 3, 2 dc in the beginning sp; *ch 3, skip the next ch-2 sp, tr3tog cluster in the next 3 dc; ch 3, skip the next ch-4 sp, tr3tog cluster in the next 3 dc; ch 3, skip the next ch-2 sp**, (3 dc, ch 3, 3 dc) in the next ch-3 sp*; repeat from * to * 8 times, then repeat from * to **; 3 dc in the beginning sp; ch 1, hdc in the 3rd ch of the beginning ch.

RND 9: Ch 3 *(this equals dc)*, 3 dc in the beginning sp, *(no ch-4 here)* sc in the next ch-3 sp; [ch 4, sc in next ch-3 sp] 2 times; *(no ch-4 here)* **(4 dc, ch 4, 4 dc) in the next ch-3 sp*; repeat from * to * 8 times, then repeat from * to **; 4 dc in the beginning sp; ch 4, sl st in the 3rd ch of the beginning ch. Fasten off.

Make the second Flutter Sleeve in the same way. Weave in the ends, and block.

String

To match the delicacy of the sleeves, I prefer the braid string type (page 138). Make two braids, each 18" (45.5cm) in length or to taste. With the right side facing, slip the header of the Flutter Sleeve over the header of the dress sleeve. Matching up the header holes, weave the string in and out through both thicknesses. You can position the string ends to come out wherever you like, at the top of the arm or at the underside of the arm. Do the same with the other sleeve.

resources

MASTER KEY FOR STITCH SYMBOL DIAGRAMS

STITCH KEY

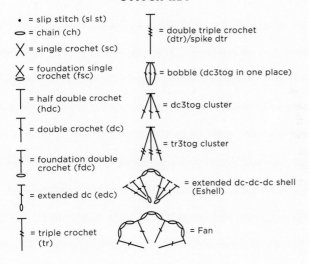

- • = slip stitch (sl st)
- ⌒ = chain (ch)
- ✕ = single crochet (sc)
- ✕ = foundation single crochet (fsc)
- T = half double crochet (hdc)
- † = double crochet (dc)
- † = foundation double crochet (fdc)
- † = extended dc (edc)
- ‡ = triple crochet (tr)
- ┬ = double triple crochet (dtr)/spike dtr
- ◊ = bobble (dc3tog in one place)
- ⋀ = dc3tog cluster
- ⋀ = tr3tog cluster
- = extended dc-dc-dc shell (Eshell)
- = Fan

Abbreviations

ch chain, chain stitch
ch- refers to a chain or space previously made
ch-sp chain space
Cl cluster
dc double crochet
dc2tog double crochet two stitches together
dtr double triple crochet
hdc half double crochet
lp(s) loop, loops
patt pattern, patterns
rnd(s) round, rounds
RS right side
sc single crochet
sc2tog single crochet two together
sl st slip stitch
sp space
st stitch
tch turning chain
tbl through the back loop
tfl through the front loop
tog together
tr triple or treble crochet
WS wrong side
YO yarn over

Strings

Crocheted strings are sturdy, decorative, practical, and practicable. They are used throughout the designs in this book to draw, gather, and close necklines, waistlines, and sleeve ends and to attach add-ons to a garment edge. Strings may be crocheted with the same yarn used in the garment. These constructions will create strong strings even if the yarn is not sturdy as a single strand; see stress test (page 138; see "Crocheted Buttons").

Choose a string type to complement the thickness of the yarn, the application, and your taste. Make strings to the length needed, generally to the measurement of your desired finished waist, neck, or arm, plus enough extra length to tie the ends, but at least as long as the measurement of the finished header. For skirts I usually do 45" to 50" (114 to 127cm) strings, but you can make them however long you please.

A good idea is to check the string on your body as you go. A great idea is to make the string longer than you think you'll need and leave a long tail for adding on later just in case you have miscalculated to avoid the aggravation of having to start all over. You can always undo extra length.

Rope

This construction makes a smooth, rounded string that slides easily through the holes. It does stretch somewhat and may curl. Use the same or one size smaller hook as used with the yarn in the garment. It is the most time-consuming type to crochet and difficult to alter for length after the fact. Try to make each sl st to the same size as the chains for the least curling and most even appearance.

Instructions

STEP 1: Make chains for entire length required, keeping chs as even as possible and relaxed enough to work into during next step.

Do not turn, but work back across the length with the front of the chains (the heart-shaped loops) facing.

STEP 2: Inserting the hook under two loops (through the face of the chain and under the nub at the back, under both strands) each time, sl st in the next ch from the hook, sl st in each ch across, fasten off.

Left to right: rope, braid, soutache

Braid

This construction makes a textured string like a tiny, slightly flattened braid. It is the stretchiest of the types here and also the most delicate. You may switch to a smaller hook than used in the garment to keep the braid more compact. It is much easier to adjust for length than the previous Rope type and is my favorite for that reason.

Instructions

STEP 1: Ch 2, sc in the 2nd ch from the hook (the first chain made); do not turn.

STEP 2: Ch 1, insert the hook from top to bottom in the front loop only of the previous sc; sc in front loop only; do not turn.

Repeat Step 2 for length desired. Fasten off.

Soutache

This construction makes a narrow, oval braid that is the thickest, most substantial of the three types here, with very little stretch, and an excellent choice for making sturdy strings from very fine or delicate yarns. Soutache in thick yarn becomes more of a skinny belt. It is easily the most decorative, but it is also the trickiest to crochet. If your gauge is too tight you will never be able to locate and work the two strands indicated. Use the same size or a size larger hook than used with the yarn in the garment.

Instructions

The braid is crocheted back and forth in rows and must be turned in the same direction each time for the pattern to work, clockwise. Keeping the hook, the loop on hook, and the feeder in place, twist just the braid as you would turn the pages of a book.

STEP 1: Ch 2, sc in 2nd ch from hook (the first chain made), turn.

If you trace the top loops of the sc just made back into the stitch, you will see a strand or nub. Technically this is a strand of the second chain made in Row 1. For the next row only you will work in the one strand at this edge.

STEP 2: Insert hook from top to bottom in the single nub at the front edge of the sc just made, sc, turn.

Now if you trace the top loops of the sc just made back into the stitch, you will see a nub at the front edge containing two strands. Technically, this is one strand of the stem and one strand of the top of the sc 2 rows below.

STEP 3: Insert the hook from top to bottom in the 2 strands of the nub at the front edge of the row, sc; turn.

Repeat Step 3 for length desired, fasten off.

Button Bridge

Soutache, with a little loop on each end, makes a terrific connector between two buttons. This tiny belt may be substituted for the string ties in the cardi styling of T-Bird Four Ways (page 106).

Instructions

LOOP AND STEP 1: Ch 6, sc in the 6th ch from the hook (in the first ch made); turn.

STEP 2: Work Soutache Step 2.

STEP 3: Work Soutache Step 3, and repeat for the length required.

ENDING LOOP: Ch 5; insert hook in the nub at the front edge as if to make Soutache Step 3, and sl st to close loop. Fasten off.

Buttons
CROCHETED BUTTONS

To survive the construction of crocheted buttons, the yarn must be sturdy enough, so before you begin, do the stress test: Take a length of the yarn you are considering for buttons, one end in one hand, one end in the other. Yank the hell out of it. If the strand breaks easily, forget about using it for buttons. If the yarn resists breaking even after lots of strong yanking, then proceed. The best outcome is for the yarn to withstand any stress applied using normal human strength.

For buttons that hold their size and stand up to wear, these are worked by crocheting around plastic bone rings.

Flat Style

This button is best for thicker or textured yarns. It puts less stress on the fiber, so might be a good choice for less sturdy yarns. If made with the same yarn and ring diameter, a flat button will be larger in diameter than a gathered button.

RND 1: With yarn and appropriate size hook, leaving several inches of beginning tail, ch 2, 7 sc in the 2nd ch from the hook (the first ch made). Work over the beginning tail as you go; sl st in the beginning sc—7 sc; do not turn.

Remove the last loop from the hook, pass the loop from back to front through the center of the ring, leaving the tail and the feeder yarn to the back of the work. The ring of sc should nearly fill the center of the plastic ring. At the front of the sc center and the plastic ring, replace the loop on the hook.

RND 2: Picking up the feeder yarn from behind the plastic ring, ch 1; working in the top loops of the sc and around the ring each time, 3 sc in each sc around, enclosing the ring in stitches—21 sc. *Do not close the round or fasten off yet.* Cut the feeder yarn, leaving several inches of tail (in case you want to turn this into a gathered button); draw up the last loop made and pull the tail all the way through. For a nearly invisible join between the first and last sc of the round, thread the tail on a tapestry needle, loop the tail around the top of the beginning sc, and sew from top to bottom back down through the top of the last sc.

I think the flat button is more interesting with the wrong side of the sc edge facing, but you may choose whichever side you want to be the front. To complete a flat button, weave ending tail neatly into back side of button, snip off close to surface.

FINISHING: Thread the beginning tail on a tapestry needle; if necessary bring the tail through the center to the back side of the button, pull it gently to tighten the center, then weave in the end, taking a few stitches at least once around the center to hide the sewing in the sc of Rnd 2. Use the remaining length of tail to attach the button to the garment.

Gathered Style

Best for finer yarns and smaller holes, this construction gathers the stitches of the flat button to the back of the ring. The resulting button is a plump doughnut with a smooth finish.

RNDS 1 AND 2: Work the same way as Rnds 1 and 2 for the flat button, making sure you leave several inches of tail before cutting the yarn and joining the sc round. Leave the ending tail for now.

The wrong side of the sc will be the front or public side of the button. Bring the beginning tail (the other tail) to the back side of the button and secure it in the same way as finishing the flat button. Leave that tail and return to the ending tail.

It is important to make buttons that are the correct size for the holes or loops in your garment, so always do a test button and check the fit. Buttons should be big enough so they don't slip out of the hole, but neither should they be so large that fastening them is impossible. If your test button isn't working for whatever reason, then go to purchased buttons.

Plastic bone rings are available at craft stores and come in several standard diameters. The most appropriate rings for the gauges in this book are from ¾" (2cm) to 1" (2.5cm) in diameter. If the pattern does not offer or suggest a button or ring size for the design, and you want to make crocheted buttons, use your judgment. Obviously once you crochet around a ring, the resulting diameter will be slightly larger than the ring. Choose a ring that will give you the button that best matches the yarn and gauge of the garment.

Unlike the relaxed gauges used in garments, crocheted buttons look best if they are worked really tightly. I suggest using a hook one or two sizes smaller than that suggested for the garment and yanking each stitch firmly.

Position button on the garment edge where desired and use the tails to attach or sew securely, or increase your options by making button studs below.

Thread the ending tail on a tapestry needle. Hold the button with the front (the wrong side of the sc) facing. Whipstitch by inserting the needle in the front loop only (the one that lies at the very edge of the round) from back to front in every other sc around. Gently pull the end to gather the stitches to the back side of the button, with the other tail coming out of the center. Knot the two tails together securely.

BUTTON STUDS

The garments in this book are designed with integrated buttonhole opportunities. There are headers (bands with holes) or evenly spaced dc row end loops along the finished edges. To keep all of your styling options open, instead of sewing buttons onto the garment, use these double button studs, which you can move around, swap out, or not use as you please.

For the most versatility I like to pair up buttons of different styles and colors. But whatever buttons you choose, make sure at least one side of the stud fits well through the intended hole. The other side of the stud can be as large and decorative as you please, since you can use the button that fits for slipping through the garment holes.

Most of the applications here will be better served by using one flat button and one shanked button. The studs are designed to go through two or more thicknesses of a crocheted edge, which can be fairly thick; using one shanked button creates the space needed between the buttons. Make them in multiples as needed; it's great to have extras.

Purchased

Purchased button studs are simply two buttons attached to each other using heavy thread or sturdy yarn. I like Stretch Magic for this task. Holding two purchased buttons back to back, sew or loop the thread, yarn, or cord through the holes and shank in the center. Knot securely, and snip off the tails close to the knot.

Crocheted

I have not included studs made with two crocheted buttons because in my experience they are not as functional as studs made with one crocheted and one purchased button. The purchased side of the stud works better if it is flat and has holes that are big enough that the yarn ends of the crocheted side will fit through.

Thread one tail of a crocheted button onto the finest needle you can manage. Hold the purchased and crocheted buttons back to back, and sew the buttons together, going through the holes in the purchased side and through the center stitches of the crocheted side. To create a shank when the purchased button is flat, wrap the yarn tail tightly several times around the stitching between the buttons. Knot the two yarn tails together securely, weave each tail a couple of stitches into the back of the crocheted button, and snip off the tails close to the surface.

Inserting the Hook in a Chain

I want to make sure we are on the same page about this. A chain has a face, two strands that look like a little heart and resemble the top loops of other regular stitches; a chain also has a nub, or butt, one strand that is the bump behind the face. Depending on whether you are working back and forth (turning after each row) or in rounds (not turning), you could be working chains with their faces facing or their butts facing. Either way, to work in the chain, insert the hook between the two strands of the face (into the center of the heart) *and* under the nub. You will end up with one strand of the face and the butt on the hook, and one strand of the face below the hook.

Chainless Foundations

Traditionally, crochet fabric begins with a chain foundation, where you make a length of chain stitches as required, then work the first row or round of stitches in the chains. This chain foundation always seems to choke the beginning edge. Working in a chain always distorts the chains around it. Counting chains is a gruesome task.

For garments that require stretch, elasticity, and stability in the neckline or waistline, I recommend using a chainless foundation. The foundation single crochet (fsc) and foundation double crochet (fdc) are written into the patterns of nearly every design in this book; the use of the technique is not an option, it is a design feature.

EXTENDED STITCHES

Fsc and fdc are members of the extended stitch family. Extended stitches have an extra step in the stem, exactly like making a ch 1 before completing the usual stitch. Extended stitches are a little bit taller than their regular sister stitches.

EXTENDED SC (ESC): Insert the hook in the next st as directed, YO and draw up a loop, YO and draw through one loop on the hook (in other words, ch 1), YO and draw through the 2 loops on the hook.

EXTENDED DC (EDC): YO, insert the hook in the next st as directed, YO and draw up a loop, YO and draw through one loop on hook (in other words, ch 1), [YO and draw through 2 loops on hook] 2 times.

Foundation Single Crochet (fsc)

What you're making is a very narrow strip equivalent to a row of sc running along one edge, each with its own corresponding chain running along the other edge. Each fsc is an extended single crochet made in the ch 1 at the base of the previous extended single crochet.

FOR THE FIRST STITCH: Begin with a slip knot on the hook. Ch 2, insert the hook in the 2nd chain from the hook (in other words in the first chain made), YO and draw up a loop (2 loops on the hook), YO and draw through one loop on the hook. (This is the ch 1 part.) Try not to yank on this chain, because you will have to find it and work into it in the next step. I tell people to pinch the ch 1 and hold it. YO and draw through the 2 loops on the hook. This is exactly like making an extended single crochet in the first chain.

The foundation will hang down from the hook, rotating so that it is almost upside down. The sc stitches will be to the hook side and below. The chains will be to the nonhook side and on top. The idea is to insert the hook so that you leave two strands of chain along the nonhook-side edge.

FOR THE FOLLOWING STITCHES: Insert the hook in the ch 1 step at the base of the previous stitch, through the face and under the nub (leaving two strands at the nonhook side), YO and draw up a loop (the ch 1), YO and draw through the 2 loops on the hook (the sc). Repeat for the number of foundation stitches required.

Foundation Double Crochet (fdc)

Foundation double crochet is just like foundation single crochet, only wider. Each fdc is an extended double crochet made in the ch 1 at the base of the previous extended double crochet.

FOR THE FIRST STITCH: Begin with a slip knot on the hook. Ch 4. Three of those chains count as the first stitch; the fourth chain from the hook is the chain at the base of the stitch.

FOR THE SECOND STITCH: YO, insert the hook in the fourth chain from the hook (in other words in the first chain made), YO and draw up a loop (3 loops on the hook), YO and draw through 1 loop on the hook. This is the ch 1 part. Try not to yank on this chain because you will have to find it and work into it in the next step. I tell people to pinch the ch 1 and hold it. [YO and draw through 2 loops on the hook] 2 times. This is exactly like making an extended double crochet in the first chains.

FOR THE FOLLOWING STITCHES: YO, insert the hook in the ch 1 step at the base of the previous stitch, through the face and under the nub, leaving two strands at the nonhook side, YO and draw up a loop (the ch 1), [YO and draw through 2 loops on the hook] 2 times. Repeat for the number of foundation stitches required.

WORKING WITH CHAINLESS FOUNDATIONS

To work fsc (fdc) as a flat foundation, turn the strip over so that the sc (dc) edge is on the top, with the last loop on the hook in the proper position to begin the next row of stitches. What you will see running along the top looks exactly like the reverse side of a row of regular sc (dc).

To connect fsc (fdc) into a ring, pick up the beginning end of the foundation and bring it up to meet the last loop on the hook. Be super careful that the stitches are not twisted. For fsc, sl st in the top loops of the first fsc you made; for fdc, the first stitch is the top of the beginning ch 4. Then continue working along the sc (dc) edge. What you will see running along the top looks exactly like the front side of a row of regular sc (dc) stitches.

To work the chain edge of fsc, rotate the piece so that the chain edge is on top. Each chain is an entire chain, not simply the spare loop of a chain, and has three strands. You may choose to work across the chain edge by inserting the hook under any or all of the strands, but I prefer to work under the entire chain edge, all three strands each time.

To work the chain edge of fdc, I prefer to insert the hook under the two strands of chain, the way I would work in a regular chain, through the face and under the nub at the back.

If the pattern needs you to work with fsc and fdc for specific applications, there will be instructions in the text.

BFF (Blocking Friends Forever)

Please stop cringing when you get to the end of a pattern and see the word *block*. Blocking is not an ordeal to be feared and loathed. Blocking is the yarn equivalent of good grooming. Even if your piece looks great to you straight off the hook, blocking (along with the proper weaving in of ends) takes the level of your crochet from homemade to handcrafted.

But it goes deeper than mere primping. More than just looking neater, with keener stitch definition and an overall professional finish, the lace patterns and motifs in this book need blocking in order for them to learn what their roles are in the shape of the garment. Also, some yarn fibers depend on wetting and blocking in order to be pleasant to wear, to drape well, or to reach their full potential. Some plant fibers like linen, hemp, and certain types of cotton, often as stiff as twine in the ball, reveal their soft, crisp drape only after blocking. Even yarn that is already lovely in the ball, such as good wool, mohair, and cashmere, will soften, plump, and full, or develop their characteristic halos only after blocking.

Thread crocheters know all about blocking. Many lifetimes ago when I made my first cotton thread doily, I wanted to cry because off the hook it was a sorry little crumpled mess. I found out that it takes rigorous steaming, pinning, and even starching to finish thread pieces. After block-ing that doily I wanted to cry again, the result was so beautiful and utterly rewarding. I began looking forward to blocking. Strangely, for some projects, the blocking is nearly as satisfying as the crocheting. Nearly.

Don't panic. There will be no harsh pinning or starching here. In all my years of designing I've never felt the need to do any more than what is described below. Absolutely no special tools, blocking wires, pins, mats, or screens are ever required. If you have water, some old lint-free towels (if you've got ShamWow towels, goody!), and a place roomy enough to spread out the crochet, then you're ready.

WET BLOCKING

For yarns that are water washable (see the yarn ball band for washing care), I totally recommend wet blocking. This is the same thing as "hand wash, lay flat to dry."

1   Dunk the crochet in a sink filled with cool water. You can add a drop of fragrant liquid wool wash or shampoo to the water first if you like, no rinsing needed. Get the piece totally wet. Avoid excessive wringing or twisting.

2   Drain the water, and press the piece gently to remove as much water as you can. If it's a larger project like an afghan you may put it in a washing machine and run a spin-only cycle until it's damp dry. Otherwise, roll it in towels to soak up as much moisture as possible.

3   Lay the damp piece on a roomy enough flat surface, like a moisture-tolerant table, a bed, or a clean floor covered with towels.

4   Gently but judiciously push, pull, straighten, smooth, and fuss with the fabric until the piece has the finished dimensions you want. Do not overstretch. Some yarns stretch alarmingly when wet but will pull back when dry. Some yarns actually seize and get tighter when wet, but will relax as they dry. Only experience will tell you what to expect. Just push and pat the piece back into place.

5   Allow the piece to dry completely. Drying could take hours. Drying could take days. It depends, you know?

If this level of immersion is not practical, you can do damp blocking. First, spread out your crochet on a layer of towels atop a water-resistant surface. Spray the piece with water until it is dampened, then ease it into shape and allow it to dry completely.

For really stubborn edges that won't uncurl, or to touch up the fold lines of stored garments (professional stylists routinely do this at photo shoots), you may lightly steam small areas. Do not touch the surface of the crochet with a steam iron!

Sources for Yarns and Materials

HOOKS

I designed and crocheted the yarn projects in this book exclusively with Tulip Brand Etimo Cushion Grip crochet hooks, available at retail locations and online at Buy.Caron.com.

YARNS AND MATERIALS

As of the writing of this book, all yarns and shades used in the samples are currently available at craft stores, yarn shops, and online. Please contact the companies and distributors below for a list of retailers.

Berroco, Inc.
Weekend
1 Tupperware Drive, Suite 4,
N. Smithfield, RI 02896-6815
401-769-1212

info@berroco.com

www.berroco.com

Blue Sky Alpacas, Inc.
Skinny Dyed, Spud & Chloë Fine
P.O. Box 88
Cedar, MN 55011
763-753-5815
888-460-8862

info@blueskyalpacas.com

http://blueskyalpacas.com/

Bryson Distributing
distributors of Rainbow Elastic
Eugene, OR
800-544-8992
http://www.brysonknits.com

Caron International
Etimo Hooks, Joy!, Simply Soft, NaturallyCaron.com Spa
Caron International
P.O. Box 222
Washington, NC 27889

www.caron.com

www.naturallycaron.com

buy.caron.com

Fairmount Fibers Ltd.
distributors of Manos del Uruguay yarns
P.O. Box 2082
Philadelphia, PA 19103
888-566-9970

info@fairmountfibers.com

www.fairmountfibers.com

Knitting Fever, Inc.
distributor of Elsebeth Lavold Hempathy
P.O. Box 336
315 Bayview Avenue
Amityville, NY 11701
516-546-3600

www.knittingfever.com

Kollage Yarns
Sock-a-licious
3591 Cahaba Beach Road
Birmingham, AL 35242
888-829-7758

info@kollageyarns.com

www.kollageyarns.com

Kraemer Yarns
Tatamy
P.O. Box 72
Nazareth, PA 18064-0072
800-759-5601

www.kraemeryarns.com

Misti International, Inc.
distributors of Misti Alpaca Tonos Pima Silk
P.O. Box 2532
Glen Ellyn, IL 60138-2532
888-776-9276

info@mistialpaca.com

www.mistialpaca.com

Prism Yarns
Windward Layers
info@prismyarn.com

www.prismyarn.com

South West Trading Company
Oasis
www.soysilk.com

Tahki Stacy Charles, Inc.
Tahki Cotton Classic Lite, Filatura Di Crosa Superior, Filatura Di Crosa Zara
70-60 83rd Street, Building #12
Glendale, NY 11385
718-326-4433

info@tahkistacycharles.com

www.tahkistacycharles.com

Tunney Wool Company
distributors of O-Wool Balance
915 N. 28th Street
Philadelphia, PA 19130
888-673-0260

info@tunneywoolcompany.com

www.o-wool.com

index